ROUTLEDGE LIBRARY EDITIONS:
SMALL BUSINESS

Volume 10

MARKETING IN SMALL BUSINESSES

MARKETING IN SMALL BUSINESSES

BRIAN KENNY WITH KAREN DYSON

LONDON AND NEW YORK

First published in 1989 by Routledge

This edition first published in 2016
by Routledge
2 Park Square, Milton Park, Abingdon, Oxon OX14 4RN

and by Routledge
711 Third Avenue, New York, NY 10017

Routledge is an imprint of the Taylor & Francis Group, an informa business

© 1989 Brian Kenny and Karen Dyson

All rights reserved. No part of this book may be reprinted or reproduced or utilised in any form or by any electronic, mechanical, or other means, now known or hereafter invented, including photocopying and recording, or in any information storage or retrieval system, without permission in writing from the publishers.

Trademark notice: Product or corporate names may be trademarks or registered trademarks, and are used only for identification and explanation without intent to infringe.

British Library Cataloguing in Publication Data
A catalogue record for this book is available from the British Library

ISBN: 978-1-138-67308-3 (Set)
ISBN: 978-1-315-54266-9 (Set) (ebk)
ISBN: 978-1-138-68531-4 (Volume 10) (hbk)
ISBN: 978-1-138-68534-5 (Volume 10) (pbk)
ISBN: 978-1-315-54328-4 (Volume 10) (ebk)

Publisher's Note
The publisher has gone to great lengths to ensure the quality of this reprint but points out that some imperfections in the original copies may be apparent.

Disclaimer
The publisher has made every effort to trace copyright holders and would welcome correspondence from those they have been unable to trace.

Marketing in Small Businesses

Brian Kenny
with
Karen Dyson

Routledge

London and New York

First published in 1989
by Routledge
11 New Fetter Lane, London EC4P 4EE
29 West 35th Street, New York, NY 10001

© Brian Kenny and Karen Dyson 1989

Typeset by LaserScript Ltd, Mitcham, Surrey
Printed and bound in Great Britain by
Biddles Ltd, Guildford and King's Lynn

All rights reserved. No part of this book may be reprinted or reproduced or utilized in any form or by any electronic, mechanical, or other means, now known or hereafter invented, including photocopying and recording, or in any information storage and retrieval system, without permission in writing from the publishers.

British Library Cataloguing in Publication Data

Kenny, Brian
 Marketing in small businesses.
 1. Great Britain. Marketing by small firms – Manuals
 I. Title. II. Dyson, Karen.
 658.8

ISBN 0 415 00920 0(hbk)
      0 415 00921 9(pbk)

Contents

Preface	ix
Acknowledgements	xi
List of figures	xiii
List of tables	xv

1 *Introduction* — 1
- Synopsis — 1
- The nature of marketing — 1
- The nature of the small enterprise — 2
- Marketing and the small enterprise — 4
- The future — 9
- Case study: Butterfingers — 10
- Case study: David, Cakes of Distinction — 15
- Notes — 17
- Further reading — 17

2 *Adopting a marketing orientation* — 18
- Synopsis — 18
- Definition of marketing — 18
- Identifying customer needs and wants — 19
- Links with other functions of the business — 20
- Defining the business — 21
- Providing future direction — 22
- Building an image — 24
- Marketing and the selling concept — 26
- The cost factor — 27
- Case study: Donprint — 30
- Notes — 34
- Further reading — 34

3 *Understanding the marketing environment* — 35
- Synopsis — 35

Contents

	Impact of competition	35
	Understanding customers	39
	Technology	44
	Suppliers, resellers, and distributors	48
	Government, public, and the economy	49
	Checklist	51
	Case study: Impact of house prices	52
	Case study: Industrial manufacturing and marketing	56
	Notes	63
	Further reading	63
4	**Marketing planning**	64
	Synopsis	64
	Importance of a formalized approach	64
	Forecasting demand	66
	Setting marketing objectives	67
	Deciding on the optimum strategy	68
	Benefits of going for market share	68
	Exercising controls	69
	Planning for the longer term	70
	Checklist	72
	Case study: Merrydown Cider	73
	Note	78
	Further reading	78
5	**Products and services**	79
	Synopsis	79
	Concept of the product life cycle (PLC)	79
	New product development	84
	Product positioning	87
	Estimating demand and profitability	89
	Developing the prototype	90
	Alternative sources of development	91
	Checklist	94
	Case study: Fire-Mann (Sales) Ltd	95
	Case study: Derwent Valley Foods	98
	Notes	100
	Further reading	100
6	**Pricing**	102
	Synopsis	102
	Factors affecting price	102
	New product pricing	104
	Pricing policy	105
	Competitor- and customer-oriented pricing	107

Pricing and product differentiation	108
Pricing at the going-rate	109
Checklist	111
Case study: Linn Products	111
Note	116
Further reading	116

7 Distribution — 117
Synopsis	117
Problem areas	117
Deciding on distribution channels	121
Evaluating channels of distribution	122
Checklist	123
Case study: Strida Ltd	123
Note	126
Further reading	127

8 Marketing communications — 128
Synopsis	128
Need for effective communication	128
Communication objectives	129
Developing a logical approach	129
Thinking the problem through	130
Impact of buyer needs and behaviour	133
Channels of communication	135
Message design and the communicator	138
Communications planning	143
Checklist	145
Case study: W. Jordan (Cereals)	146
Note	154
Further reading	154

9 Overseas marketing — 155
Synopsis	155
The overseas marketing decision	155
Sources of information	156
Market selection	158
Mode of entry	158
Some key problem areas	160
Capitalizing on opportunity	163
Problems of managing documentation	166
Obtaining practical help and advice	167
Contractual arrangements	169
Case study: Woods of Windsor	172
Case study: Almo-Cut	177

Contents

	Notes	179
	Further reading	179
10	*Marketing to MOD*	180
	Synopsis	180
	Problems of marketing	180
	Background	181
	MOD organization and contact points	182
	Market entry	184
	Contracts branch administration	186
	Principles and types of contract	186
	Contract conditions	187
	Contract financing	187
	Quality assurance	188
	Annex 1: EC and GATT	188
	Annex 2: contact points	189
	Case study: Airship Industries	190
	Notes	194
	Further reading	195
11	*Franchising*	196
	Synopsis	196
	Concept of franchising	196
	Franchising in the United Kingdom	197
	Opportunities for the potential franchisee	197
	Financing the franchise	200
	Points to consider	202
	Case study: Olivers	202
	Notes	205
	Further reading	205
12	*Marketing high technology*	206
	Synopsis	206
	Importance of company image	206
	Need for customer reassurance	207
	Building an acceptable image	208
	Developing a marketing framework	210
	Case study: Celltech	211
	Notes	218
	Further reading	218
	Index	219

Preface

This book was written as an introductory guide to marketing in the small business and as such, it dwells more upon the relevant applied issues and less on the many detailed concepts and techniques associated with contemporary marketing. This approach is largely considered appropriate because the smaller enterprise is blessed with little time or opportunity to absorb vast amounts of complex theories, nor does it generally have the resources to implement many of the recommended techniques therein.

The objectives of the text are simple and straightforward, a primary aim being to provide an appreciation of the nature of marketing and the benefits of its application, particularly to the smaller enterprise. Additionally, it is the intention that the reader will be stimulated to explore further the concepts and techniques, and to this end selected readings are listed at the end of each chapter.

The chapters are ordered in such a manner as to develop and build on knowledge gained from preceding material. The first four chapters are broadly based and stress the marketing-strategy issues and the need for marketing information. Not only should the reader develop an understanding of nature and the scope and limitations of marketing from these earlier chapters but also, the relevance to the individual's business experience should begin to emerge. Chapters 5 to 8 cover the more specific areas of marketing decisions relating to product, pricing, distribution, and promotion. The final four chapters are devoted to the specialist themes of international and government markets, franchising (from the potential franchisee's point of view) and high technology. These specialist chapters have been included and isolated in view of the growing importance of these markets to the small enterprise and franchising in particular, as a potential area for the business start-up.

In order to underpin the key concepts introduced in the various chapters, short case examples are included throughout the text which are largely based on the authors' previous experience with small

Preface

businesses. For reasons of confidentiality, names and specific product/market categories have been changed. However, the case studies appearing at the end of each chapter are undisguised and almost wholly based on published information. Questions set at the end of each case allow the reader to briefly analyse the various situations using concepts previously covered.

On a final note, it is worth stressing the usefulness of supplementing readings through taking advantage of the many government-sponsored schemes offering training and practical help and advice. Although it is beyond the scope of this text to produce a detailed description of such schemes, Chapter 1 contains a flavour of the moves being taken to bridge the gap between the state and the small enterprise.

Acknowledgements

The authors are indebted to the following individuals and organizations for their co-operation in the task of gathering case material:

Paul Adcock (Almo-Cut); Nick Allen (Olivers); Charles Brennan (Linn Products); Des Donohoe (Donprint); Christine Elliot (W. Jordan); Karen Evans and Jane Connolly (Butterfingers); Helen Forster (Derwent Valley Foods); Nick Green and Mark Sanders (Strida Ltd); Nicholas Greenwood (Airship Industries); Tracy Hayson (Fire-Mann (Sales) Ltd); Penny Line (Woods of Windsor Ltd); Hilda and David MacCarfrae (David Cakes of Distinction); Sue Nicholls (Celltech); Ian Hirstle and Peter Murphy of Huddersfield Polytechnic; Merrydown Wine plc (Merrydown Cider); and to the British Overseas Trade Board, the Ministry of Defence, The Financial Times Ltd; Haymarket Publication Ltd; Department of Trade and Industry; *Gifts International, Motor Boats Monthly, Garden Trade News*, and *Trident Magazine*, for permission to reproduce articles or extract information from published data. Finally, our thanks to John Oldham of Oldham's Printers Ltd, Huddersfield, for providing valuable feedback during the early stages of developing the text.

Figures

1.1	Functional organization	3
3.1	The marketing environment	36
3.2	Marketing chains: windows and/or frames	48
4.1	The marketing planning process	65
4.2	Travelway: SWOT analysis	71
4.3	Travelway: marketing plan	73
5.1	Product life cycle	80
5.2	UK washing-machine market, 1956–64	82
5.3	UK washing-machine market, 1971–82	83
5.4	Strategy over the life cycle	83
5.5	New product development programme	86
5.6	Brand and supplier positionings	88
8.1	Developing communications strategy	131
8.2	Simplified communications model	132
8.3	Promotion/communications schedule and budget (new product launch)	146
9.1	International marketing process	156
10.1	MOD/PE organization (1987)	182
12.1	Marketing framework: build-up of capability image	212

Tables

3.1	Competitor analysis	38
9.1	Examples of specific market reports and sources	159
9.2	Comparison of typical characteristics of UK export houses	161
9.3	Types of direct export entry points	162

1 Introduction

Synopsis

Customer satisfaction is the primary aim of marketing. In focusing on the future the enterprise ensures the best possible chance of attaining long-term stability and competitive standing. For the small enterprise faced with limited resources and the day-to-day pressures of business, marketing may sometimes seem an unnecessary luxury. However, as the enterprise moves along the growth cycle, the pressure for systematic planning and the associated information needs increases. The added cost of implementing the marketing function must be weighed against the possible consequences of living with a greater level of risk and uncertainty.

The nature of marketing

Marketing makes the basic assumption that customer satisfaction should be the primary aim of the business. Such satisfaction can only be achieved and sustained through the provision of competitive products or services, at competitive prices and by ensuring that communication with customers, directly or indirectly, is appropriate and effectively targeted. The marketing concept also acknowledges that in servicing the needs of the customer more effectively than competitors, the firm will optimize profitability over the longer term.

The longer-term (strategic) viewpoint provides the focal point for planning the future direction of the firm and the efficient harnessing of scarce resources towards achieving long-term goals. Although this focus will naturally enlarge the factor of uncertainty, it becomes increasingly important as the firm experiences the pains of growth.

Decisions on product development, pricing and distribution policies and promotional strategy (the marketing mix) will require support from appropriate and up-to-date information on the market(s) concerned, if the marketing planning function is to be effective. Not only

Marketing in Small Businesses

is it a question of how to respond to the various market forces in the present, but also, to attempt to predict future change and to plan marketing responses accordingly.

Problems of generalization

While marketing principles have, in general, universal acceptance, marketing practice does not readily lend itself to standardization. Unlike, say, standard accounting routines which are widely accepted and practised, marketing is very much situation-specific in that it is dependent on several factors. For example, the nature of the markets served, the growth stage of the firm, the type of products or services offered, and the quality of management.

Therefore, it is difficult to generalize regarding the application of certain marketing theories and techniques. What may be appropriate for a manufacturing company in the way of new product development procedures, will probably be inappropriate for the retailing firm. Similarly, sophisticated marketing organization theories will have little meaning for the sole-ownership enterprise, but be highly applicable to the multi-market, multi-product firm.

In the final analysis, it is for the individual organization to judge what particular theories and techniques are most relevant to the situation, although the basic concept of marketing described previously applies in most cases.

The nature of the small enterprise

Definition

There seems to be little official agreement on what constitutes a 'small business'. Various combinations of turnover, profit, and number of employees etc., have been suggested, but these classifications have proved somewhat arbitrary and thus any attempt to produce a rigid classification becomes meaningless. It seems however, that the stage of growth of the firm and the number of personnel involved in its management are probably better indicators. These factors have implications for responsibility of the individual business functions such as production, finance, sales etc., the extent to which these functions are formally (or informally) organized, and the availability of resources to support these.

For example, in the formation and early growth stages, it is common practice for the small enterprise to buy-in financial expertise and it is probably not uncommon for one person to be responsible for more than one function such as production and sales. As the burden

Introduction

of growth begins to tell, the divisions of responsibility become more apparent, and management will generally slot into the function which best serves their individual capability and/or interests, leaving gaps for others to fill.

These early signs of formalization probably represent the transition from a small to a medium-sized enterprise, although again, it may be somewhat misleading to generalize. However, it is not unreasonable to assume that the organizational structure depicted in Figure 1.1 represents the upper limit beyond which the enterprise would probably not be considered 'small'.

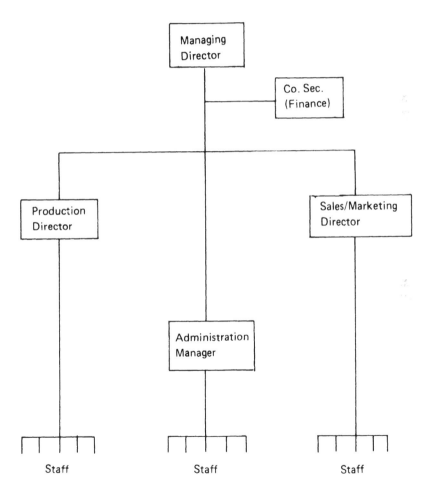

Figure 1.1 Functional organization

With further growth, through, for example, product and/or market diversification, changes in structure such as the formation of product groups or divisionalization are invariably accompanied by a relatively significant growth in number of employees and turnover.

Some facts and figures

Small enterprises are an integral and important part of the UK economy. In 1987 some 1.4 million small companies were registered for VAT in the UK and the average rate of new registrations was well over 100,000 per annum. However, past research has shown that the most critical period for the small enterprise is during the first thirty months of operation and that over a ten-year period, some 50 per cent of companies registering would have deregistered by the end of the period.

Research has also shown that unincorporated businesses such as sole proprietorships and partnerships, seem to have a better survival record in production, construction, transport, wholesale, motor trades, and other services. Companies, on the other hand, have done better in, agriculture, retailing, professional and financial services, and catering.

Marketing and the small enterprise

For the small enterprise hampered by regulatory constraints and coping with the day-to-day stresses of business, marketing theory and more so practice may at times, seem somewhat of an unnecessary luxury. It needs to be understood that if marketing is to be of any use, then time and scarce resources must be allocated to an activity which often may only show a return in the longer term. In the early stages of growth there are of course, seemingly more important activities which represent a considerable drain on resources such as the requirements of employees, purchasing, production, and financial reporting. Therefore, it is not hard to understand management's over-preoccupation with these internal considerations and, indeed, this may well be the correct strategy depending on the particular situation.

As the firm moves along the growth cycle however, a much more externally orientated view is needed which takes account of changes in competition, customer demands, the economy, and technological developments among others. As the need for a more systematic approach to business development emerges, so the necessity to cope with greater uncertainty arises and the pressure for more information,

Introduction

skill at interpretation, and commitment to higher-risk decisions, collectively increase the burden on management.

There is of course the cost factor to consider in adopting a systematic planning approach and with the drain on resources faced by most small enterprises, marketing often tends to take a back seat. None the less, it is important to consider the possible cost of ignoring the issues and the subsequent longer-term problems that may arise.

Sometimes, management may only have a subjective or at best, a limited objective assessment of growth opportunity. Often, such recognition of an opportunity is based on an internally-generated idea or actual product, with little or no evidence of likely market response. Under these circumstances the risks associated with further development investment are considerably multiplied.

Information needs

For the various marketing decisions that face the small enterprise, more often than not, information on the market has to be gathered and interpreted. The sources of information may include customers, distributors, or published data on the industry and markets concerned. For many small enterprises specializing in fairly minor sectors of the market, broad statements on the market as a whole may be of little value; therefore much of the published information on markets will have its limitations. Reliable information is essential for effective market planning and the firm may have to resort to primary market research, that is, gathering relevant information which is not already available, be it on customers or competitors.

Decisions on products, pricing, promotion, and distribution (where appropriate) require at least a reasonable understanding of the market forces at play and this point is continuously stressed in the following chapters. Occasionally, the small enterprise will not only need information for its own use, but also to convince outside-interest groups of its credibility as a viable concern, as the following case study illustrates.

Precision Engineering Services
Simon Carter commented: 'With my redundancy pay I set up a small engineering company mainly producing precision engineered components. As the orders increased I found I had to borrow to buy more machinery and the loan was secured on my house.

'About three years later when I ran into cash-flow problems

5

I approached the bank but they just didn't want to know. The irony was that the business looked so promising, it just seemed unfair that even accepting the lack of security I wasn't considered a safe bet.

'As a last resort I contacted the local authority development corporation. Although I had to provide the usual forecasts and cash flows in support of the application I found it frustrating to answer pointed questions about the market, or my competitors, or my plans for the future. In truth, I didn't have the answers at the time and of course I realize now I could hardly have expected any outsider to have shared my own faith in the business.

'Although I wasn't successful with the application I was advised to think about the issues and to re-apply at a later stage. As it happened, I had planned a weekend break in the Lake District, more for my wife's sake really. She didn't see much of me and I felt I needed to get away from the pressures of the business.

'For the first time in the three years I had been in the business I began to collect my thoughts and to view things from the longer-term aspect. Surprisingly, my wife not only listened but she actually understood and seemed keen to be involved. In the relaxed atmosphere I was able to think more objectively and by the time we'd left the hotel I, or I should say *we*, had a much clearer idea of what was needed if the business was to survive.

'Of course I had to get some professional guidance in the end, but I was much more confident and this seemed to rub off on customers. Eventually, I had a better idea of what, and who, I was up against, a much clearer view of the market, and, most important, a longer-term goal to aim for. I did get a loan after re-applying to the development corporation and looking back, I think the failure to get the money in the first instance was probably a godsend.'

Conclusion

From Simon Carter's experiences we might assume that some of the problems facing small businesses result from a failure to project credibility on the one hand and caution – or over-caution – on the other. Clearly, conviction must be on both sides of the fence, whether dealing with customers, suppliers or potential sources of finance.

While in the early stages of development, the small enterprise may be relatively confident regarding decisions that come within the scope of marketing, successive growth plans, and growth itself, will increase

Introduction

the pressure both for more understanding of the market(s) and the effectiveness of existing and/or future marketing decisions. The latter may encompass new product development, pricing, distribution, and advertising and promotion decisions, all of which may require more information than is generally at hand. For example, price sensitivity of demand, advertising effectiveness, changing customer needs, and purchasing habits or the likely market response to a new product launch.

In contemporary business, sustaining success is largely to do with being competitive and this requires the enterprise to be aware of the behaviour of the market or markets, that it serves. While it may be tempting to reject the notion of gathering and interpreting information purely on economic grounds, the consequences could prove far more costly in the longer term. Certainly, it appears that marketing information and consultancy services are gradually coming within the pockets of smaller businesses and that such support is high on the list of government priorities:

> The Enterprise Initiative announced last week by Lord Young, the Enterprise Secretary, promises a brave new world for Britain's smaller companies. Little in the proposals is really new, but the government has provided much more money for a number of well-proven ideas, such as the subsidy of management consultancy.
> The initiative attempts to overcome a particular hurdle facing any government attempt to get closer to small business. In the past the small-business owner has distrusted Whitehall as a source of finance or advice, convinced that civil servants do not understand his problems and that any help will be tied up in red tape.
> The decision to create a network of offices around the country to provide counselling and, if required, referral to a professional management consultant, should overcome this reluctance to deal with government directly.
> This network of offices – twenty-seven new ones are planned alongside the Department of Enterprise's existing seven regional offices – will also add to the existing range of services available to small firms through the three hundred-plus Enterprise Agencies and the ten Small Firms Service Offices run by the Department of Employment.
> Will the small businessman know where to go for advice? The answer is that the start-up or early-stage company in need of advice should approach its local Enterprise Agency or Small Firms Service office.

Marketing in Small Businesses

The Enterprise Agencies provide advice in an informal manner while the Small Firms offices give three sessions of free counselling followed by up to ten further sessions at £30 each.

The larger company which is already established but now wants to expand should apply to an enterprise counsellor in one of the Department of Trade and Industry offices. Many of the new 'satellite offices' will be based in Enterprise Agencies or chambers of commerce.

The new enterprise counsellors will give two days of free advice and assessment. If they think the problem justifies it they will recommend the use of professional management consultants. The government will meet half of the cost of advice for up to fifteen days though the subsidy rises to two-thirds in the assisted, and urban programme areas.

If the businessman is not quite sure to which office to apply, he should approach either one. He will then be referred to the appropriate local office. This referral involves a simple form giving details of name and address. The form will be sent to the local office which is best suited to deal with the case and its staff will make contact with the businessman.

A problem which will undoubtedly arise is whether enough new enterprise counsellors of sufficient quality can be found. The Small Firms Service already has more than three hundred of its own counsellors in England dealing with 25,000 cases a year.

The number of qualified businessmen who are not already involved in running their own business or who retain, in retirement, the ability to solve the problems of small business, is clearly limited. There are already plans to use some of the Small Firms counsellors in the enterprise counselling programme.

There is also the question of whether there are enough management consultants available with an understanding of the special problems of small business to supply the 1,000 consultancy projects Lord Young envisages will take place each month over the next few years.

That said, the idea of providing subsidised consultancy advice is likely to prove very popular. The Support for Marketing scheme launched in September 1986 met with such demand that the government was forced to more than double the £2.5 million initially allocated to it.

Marketing is one of the four subject areas previously covered by subsidised consultancy schemes to be picked up by the Enterprise Initiative. The others are design, quality management, and manufacturing methods and systems.

The sorts of problems the marketing consultants will look at include market studies to see how customers' demands are changing and examinations of pricing, distribution, and after-sales service.

The design consultants, for example, might look at areas such as design for efficient production, materials selection, and product safety.

Two new areas of consultancy advice will be introduced in April. They are business planning, to help companies control costs, lift profits and raise new finance, and financial and information systems to allow companies to improve budget and financial control, maintain accounting records, and decide on their computer and software needs.

Lord Young also promises a reorganization of the British Overseas Trade Board better to reflect exporters' needs. The BOTB last year announced a revamp of its service to provide more targeted advice to the non-exporter and to call on outside exporting expertise so it is difficult to see what still needs to be done. A DTI spokeswoman described the plan as 'a repackaging' of the existing programme.

One part of the enterprise initiative which may make an impact only in the long term is a plan to encourage teachers to gain commercial work experience. Various programmes to expose school children and undergraduates to the idea of self-employment have been tried in recent years but teachers are frequently unenthusiastic about schemes which involve pupils running their own minibusinesses.[1]

The future

At the time of writing much government publicity was being levelled at the creation of a single European Market by the year 1992. Such a change would bring both threats and opportunities for many small enterprises and almost certainly, the need for a greater awareness of marketing and its practice.

The removal of national barriers and the eventual imposition of European standards would likely affect a wide range of products and Britain could not afford to be left out of the process of agreement. Failure to comply with new requirements would obviously make it difficult, if not impossible, to sell within Europe. Many changes had already been agreed by 1988 and 1992 would see completion of the legislation programme.

Predicting the impact of such change and planning suitable courses of action is an integral part of marketing. While the change would bring new opportunities it would also bring the threat of increased

Marketing in Small Businesses

competition in the home market and, therefore, the planning function should give equal consideration to these factors.

There is little doubt that enthusiasm, conviction, and diligence are hardly ever wanting in the smaller enterprise and that these characteristics are essential ingredients for success – accepting of course, that adequate financial resources are ever-present! In adding a marketing orientation to these qualities the enterprise can considerably enhance its competitive stance and, along with the proverbial element of luck, improve the chances of long-term survival.

The following short cases demonstrate that, even for the very small enterprise, the above comments have some credence and, in the chapters following, their implications will be further expanded and explored.

Case study: Butterfingers

In 1988 Butterfingers food bar was awarded its sixth consecutive entry in Egon Ronay's *Just a Bite* food guide – quite an accolade for a small, but dynamic, enterprise, situated in the heart of industrial east Lancashire. Butterfingers' entry in the guide was as follows:

> This simple, pine-panelled cafe makes a pleasantly informal setting for Jane Connolly and Karen Evans' enjoyable hot and cold dishes. At any time of day there are excellent fresh salads with home-made mayonnaise, savoury flans, filled jacket potatoes and daily specials like cauliflower cheese and moussaka, plus assorted sandwiches. Sweets include crisp ginger biscuits, buttery shortbread and delicious apple pie.

The business owners had been friends since schooldays and at the time the business idea was conceived in 1980, both women were in their late twenties and settled into married life. Karen Evans, who had advanced qualifications in catering and was employed as a school meals supervisor, was looking for a more challenging occupation, while Jane Connolly who had two young children, was keen to see a more formal set-up arising from the casual, outside catering business each had been involved with for a short period of time. The partners had been doing catering for friends' parties and they had been motivated to develop the business to a large extent, by the favourable response received from this spare-time activity. Fortunately, they had the backing of their husbands, who were both professional men and eager to see the business idea develop and succeed. Karen's husband, Bob, was accommodations officer for a large educational establishment in the north-west. Jane's husband, Paul, had his own building contractor business, which was to prove invaluable for the

Karen Evans and Jane Connolly (photo copyright: R. Evans, 1988).

Marketing in Small Businesses

setting up of the new premises and for subsequent interior alteration work.

Although other sites had been considered, the main search for premises ended in the partners' home town of Burnley, Lancashire. While it was considered that a location in the main shopping area was obviously desirable, the cost of rent and rates seemed prohibitive, particularly as capital was sorely needed for equipment and fittings. A £20,000 business development loan had been secured from the National Westminster Bank and it was the partners' intention to pay outright for capital items needed rather than resort to lease or hire purchase. Eventually, suitable premises close to the centre of town and just off the main high street, became available and although rent and rates were lower than for the prime sites, they were none the less barely affordable.

Jane's husband was able to take responsibility for the design and fitting out of the premises and the business development loan went largely towards the purchase of fixtures and catering equipment and facilities. The business was formally opened in May 1981 under the name Uppercrust as a take-away food shop. Items on the menu included: boeuf bourguignon, lasagne, chilli con carne, spaghetti bolognese, blanquette of pork, and to add a touch of local colour, Lancashire hot pot plus other home-made delicacies, in addition to a range of freshly prepared sandwiches and sweets. The shop initially catered for just fifteen sit-down customers but on the first few days of opening, it became obvious that demand had been underestimated. The partners, however, could do little about this given the limitations of the overall size of the shop premises. There was some feeling that perhaps the opening promotional campaign had gone a little overboard. Karen Evans explained:

> 'For the evening before the opening day we had hired a local club and had sent out invitations to a wide range of local businesses, including solicitors, banks, building societies, shops, the town hall and others that we considered to be potential sources of business. On the actual evening we were quite astounded as about 350 guests turned up. Anyway, we served them samples of our home-made cooking and the response seemed favourable. The following week we had a full page advertisement – supplier-sponsored – in the local newspaper.'

In spite of the early success of the venture, the business was to have its first major problem. It transpired that a firm of outside caterers had for some time been using the name Uppercrust and within six weeks of the shop opening, the partners were facing court action. As a desperate measure the shop changed its name to Uppercrunch but

Introduction

the county court judge granted an interim injunction preventing the shop from trading under either name, on the basis that 'the new name could be mistaken for the original firm'. Jane Connolly commented: 'It just seemed ridiculous at the time. We weren't a threat to the company during those early days and we gathered they weren't doing much business anyway – and we didn't even know they existed.'

As it happened, a change of name to *Butterfingers* had little or no effect on the ultimate progress of the business and as a result of the publicity of the court action, many customers had expressed concern and sympathy regarding their predicament and in Karen's words: 'Even this publicity was probably to the benefit of our company although we had to pay costs of £800 to the other company in the end.' The shop also had to bear the cost of producing new publicity material and stationery, etc.

The second major problem came about two years after opening when profitability and cash-flow improvement seemed to have reached a plateau, if not taken a turn for the worse. As Karen explained: 'I think at the time we both were prepared to sell off the business and it was very easy to get demoralized.' However, during a visit to their accountant, it was suggested that the products were probably underpriced and that prices should be increased if they were to have a better chance of remaining in business. Karen admitted:

> 'We were mainly trying to undercut what we regarded as competition: for example, other sandwich shops and hot meal providers such as cafes and fast food outlets. Actually, it had taken us about twelve months to get the product line right. In adjusting to customer requirements we had greatly reduced the initial variety of offerings, although we still provided a wide choice. What we hadn't quite appreciated was the price/quality relation- ship nor had we really understood the market at which we were aiming.'

On advice from the accountant the prices were increased and fortunately the existing customer base didn't react too adversely and the business was restored to a satisfactory level of profitability within a relatively short period of time.

As the business developed, Butterfingers expanded into outside catering and in 1987 seating capacity was increased to seat twenty-one persons. Also, in 1988 the interior of the shop was re-designed to facilitate counter service, minimizing inconvenience to the eat-in side. Over this period, products and services had been fine-tuned to the market with new menu items coming from a variety of sources. On one occasion while on a visit to the Lake District, Karen and husband Bob came across a very interesting sweet dish with the very unrevealing title of 'sticky toffee pudding'. Karen couldn't quite work out the

Marketing in Small Businesses

formula within the short time they were there, so Bob later wrote to the cafe – Sheila's Cottage in Ambleside – and for his gall received a friendly reply *and* the recipe! The pudding was subsequently added to the Butterfingers menu and proved very successful!

Jane, being a very competent cook and having an eye for customer needs, also actively contributed to new product development and service improvements. Jane's outgoing nature and pleasant manner had helped develop a strong, loyal customer base which itself has considerably influenced the nature of the business. Regular customers were often asked to try new or improved products, before these were formally added to the menu.

With regard to promotion, only limited use had been made of media advertising. In Karen's words: 'Apart from the opening promotion and regular reporting of our Egon Ronay recommendation, we have not made too much use of advertising. The business has been built up on the basis of customer satisfaction and word-of-mouth communication.'

Both Karen and Jane felt that the business – although there was potential for growth – was about the right size. Neither partner for various reasons, wished to devote more effort. Indeed, in early 1988 they decided to leave the running of the shop on Saturdays, to a full-time member of staff. Caroline Mossop had been with Butterfingers almost since its opening, joining the business through the Youth Opportunities Scheme. With her expertise and knowledge of the business gained over the years, she could efficiently cope with the customers and manage the part-time staff at this busy period, with relative ease. This allowed both partners to take a well-earned rest at weekends and to spend more time with their respective families.

In 1987 Karen decided to advance her education in the hospitality field and she embarked upon an HCIMA diploma course at Manchester Polytechnic. This was to take her away from the business for another full day each week and it seemed that the thirst for challenge was again in the air. For Jane, the existing business to some extent represented an outlet for activity and she was content to continue, but not beyond the present level. For Karen however, the long term was likely to mean a change of direction. She explained:

'I doubt if I will be in this particular business in five to ten years time. We could grow, but neither of us really wants this. Jane is content putting in the time, but she doesn't want to devote more than she is doing and I appreciate her feelings. For myself I'd like to do something else; run a small hotel possibly. I'm enjoying the HCIMA course and particularly Marketing – it's interesting yet it's so obvious, really. At least it's obvious to me now, looking at it from an academic viewpoint.'

Introduction

Karen admitted however, that things weren't that obvious seven years ago. Twelve months to get the menu properly organized and in line with market needs and almost two years before the pricing was finally sorted out. During this initial period, things could very well have gone either way. The partners had recognized a gap in the market, but the initial lack of both understanding of, and appropriate information on, market needs, had resulted in things being left very much to chance.

Case study: David, Cakes of Distinction[2]

The sweet taste of success grows apace for the enterprising mother and son team who successfully saw off the opposition in the Merseyside heat of Granada Television's *Flying Start* business programme, in 1988, to take the county first prize and £10,000 in cash. Orders are now tumbling through the door of their shop and bakery in Crosby village and pinned-up thank you letters from Buckingham and Holyrood Palaces ensure a constant stream of bemused and astonished passers-by, peeking through the windows at the array of displays that have made David, Cakes of Distinction, something of a household name in confectionery circles.

In a little less than three years, Hilda and David MacCarfrae have broken into what they described as a moribund market and given it a right good shaking up. Customers have included Granada, who wanted a birthday cake for the tenth anniversary of the *Krypton Factor*; Yorkshire Television, who brought in the artistic skills of 23-year-old David to hype up its party for *Emmerdale Farm*'s birthday; and British Rail who spurned Travellers Fare in favour of David and had him create a lavish cake to mark their InterCity coming of age this summer.

But the pinnacle of their meteoric rise to fame in the essentially conservative confectionery world came with the commission to prepare one of the twenty-one cakes for the wedding bash of the Duke and Duchess of York in July 1986.

Their high-profile attack on the market has ensured a regular dose of publicity and business magazines and local press have beaten a path to their door for a slice of the action. And recently they were highlighted in the *Sunday Times* small business story section. The tale was first told in *Trident*, but they deserve a second helping due to Hilda MacCarfrae's ambitious plans to develop the business. They intend to open a school for training would-be confectioners where David can pass on his skills and ensure the continued success of their own retailing arm. Already she has found suitable premises, a mere stone's throw from their bright and airy shop, which she says should be ready for the first intake in January 1988: 'We discovered that

Marketing in Small Businesses

David MacCarfrae (photo copyright: Geoff Roberts)

there is a tremendous shortage of confectioners and hardly any training courses. So we decided to set up our own school.'

They have picked up a tutor to help David who will take students through to City and Guilds standard and David has already begun a teaching programme. Apart from their own eight staff, he has spent six weeks putting on a part-time course for thirty keen confectioners in the tiny bakery above the shop: 'The demand is there and we decided to go ahead with the idea of a full-time school.' In the meantime he is also keen to get to grips with another project. Like all good cooks, he is an artist and believes there is a need for a specialist book on confectionery techniques: 'It's a dream at the moment, but I will get round to realizing it in time.'

Winning ways

David MacCarfrae had studied the confectioner's art in Switzerland, following two years as a baker in Hertford. While abroad he recognized that there was room for innovation in the UK. Hilda MacCarfrae admits to 'getting in where angels fear to tread' and having a 'particular skill in marketing'. Early success followed from a demonstration in a Southport hotel where, Hilda commented: 'We brought in fifteen orders worth more than £1,000 in a single day and realized we'd found a special niche in the market.'

Notes

1 *Financial Times*, 19 January 1988 (reproduced by kind permission of Financial Times Ltd).
2 *Trident Magazine*, Merseyside Chambers of Commerce, September 1987, 21.

Further Reading

Lewis, J. et al. (eds) (1984) *Success and Failure in Small Businesses*, Aldershot: Gower.

2 Adopting a marketing orientation

Synopsis

In adopting a true marketing orientation, the firm attempts to direct its efforts towards satisfying customer needs in a competitive manner. This action is designed to ensure, as far as possible, long-term survival rather than short-term profitability per se, and it requires the firm to think beyond the immediate future. An essential part of the process is the building of an appropriate image in the eyes of existing and potential customers such that they will be more favourably disposed to the firm. For the small business, the cost of adopting a complete marketing profile may seem prohibitive, but this should always be weighed against the consequences of opting for the lower-cost alternative of working with very limited marketing information. In the end, it is up to the firm to decide with what degree of uncertainty it can reasonably cope and therefore where its marketing resources can best be deployed.

Definition of marketing

Contemporary marketing has its roots in the early market-trading systems, around which many towns and cities worldwide have expanded and developed. It is basically an exchange process in which the seller and the buyer seek mutual satisfaction. This exchange process is generally thought of as a goods- or services-for-money commercial transaction, although nowadays, many public sector bodies and other non-profit-making organizations have adopted certain marketing-based techniques in order to improve efficiency.

In the present highly industrialized and intensely competitive scene, marketing has expanded its previous limited boundaries to encompass sophisticated research and analytical techniques along with theories and applications from the social sciences. However, the modern *concept* is relatively simple to understand and in essence, is no more than common sense would have us believe. Although there are a number of formal definitions in existence they are basically in agreement on the following points:

- The firm should be prepared to identify customer needs and wants
- With the above in mind, the firm should adapt its operations to achieving customer satisfaction in a manner which gives the firm a distinct competitive edge

Although the exchange process is not explicitly stated in this definition, the implication is that customer satisfaction equals profitability and if the firm can deliver more satisfaction than its competitors, the greater the profit potential. In other words the concept relies on the adoption of a customer orientation.

Identifying customer needs and wants

The above philosophy represents the starting point for grasping all of the underlying principles and practices concerned with marketing, even if for the small business its actual application may present particular problems. While a customer orientation may seem obvious, it can be argued that some sectors of British industry seem to have been slow to grasp its importance, for reasons which will become clear later. In order to meet customer needs and wants, these must first be understood. It is this understanding which seems to cause problems; not only because needs are sometimes difficult and expensive to research but also, because many firms often adopt a rather complacent attitude towards their customers. The resulting symptoms may show up in a variety of guises such as an over-obsession with the product or service being offered, aggressive selling, arrogance on the part of the seller, or simple ignorance of the customer needs.

Sometimes we think we know what the customer needs and therefore we see no point in taking the matter further. This feeling is often accompanied by a conviction that what we have to offer is really better than our competitors whether it be product quality, price, after-sales-service, or some combination of these factors. It is only when the business starts losing sales to competitors the realization sets in that all is not well and panic measures are often taken, with little or no understanding of the underlying causes of the problem.

Focusing on customer needs and therefore adopting a customer orientation really costs very little. It is an approach which moves away from the tangible product or service and focuses on the benefits the customer accrues from the adoption of the product or service. It is

Marketing in Small Businesses

really a question of the supplier putting himself in the shoes of the customer and trying to understand what particular needs are being sought. As an example and firstly looking at the problem from the supplier end, consider three relatively well known organizations: IBM, Polaroid, and Bird's Eye. If we posed the question 'What do these companies sell?' the answers would probably be computers, cameras (and films) and frozen foods, respectively.

Yet when we pose the question, 'What are the customers actually buying?' the answers are less obvious. Firstly, the potential IBM customer would probably be concerned with how the computer could increase the efficiency of processing data within the company, provide accurate and up-to-date information, and generally improve business operations. The Polaroid camera purchaser, unlike, say, the Pentax enthusiast would probably see the benefits as simple-to-use, efficient way of recording and instantly viewing, generally happy events which can also be referred to at some future date. The customer for Bird's Eye frozen foods could well be the busy wife seeking a quick method of organizing meals for the family while avoiding the drudge of preparing from scratch. Using this simple analysis we now could re-phrase our answers to the original question 'What do the following companies sell?'

- IBM: business efficiency
- Polaroid: instant memories
- Bird's Eye: convenience

We could of course expand on these rather simplified definitions but at least they serve to show the focus on the consumer, rather than on the actual product. This simple, but effective way of looking at the problem is paramount to understanding the marketing concept, for it puts the emphasis on customer needs and benefits. Whatever business the firm happens to be in it is worth pondering over these factors and attempting to put oneself in the position of customers. With regard to the latter it is worth posing the following questions:

- What are they really buying?
- What benefits do they seek?
- How well do the firm's competitors meet these needs and perceived benefits?
- How well does the firm compare with competitors in the light of the answers to the above questions?

Links with other functions of the business

As marketing suggests a customer focus for the firm's activities it

Adopting a marketing orientation

seems logical that, according to the nature of the firm, it should provide direction for other functions of the business such as finance, production and personnel. Clearly, no function can work in isolation, yet it is not impossible for conflict to arise between these divisions of responsibility and even more so in the absence of proper management guidelines. It is not uncommon for individuals to set their own objectives and values as they think fit, as the following examples illustrate:

- 'My job is to ensure that production runs smoothly and is evenly scheduled' (production manager).
- 'I am here to ensure that nobody goes over budget' (financial manager).
- 'To get the best possible sales figures every month is my main objective' (sales manager).
- 'I see my main responsibility as ensuring good industrial relations and job satisfaction' (personnel manager).

There may be nothing wrong with such objectives, except that with a lack of a common aim and overall co-ordination, conflict is likely to arise. For example, the best possible sales figures may not be conducive to smooth and even production nor even to ensuring job satisfaction among salesmen or production operatives.

An effective customer orientation must by necessity, have at least an overriding market-based aim to which the above sub-objectives can relate in harmony. For example:

- To be a respected supplier of high-quality products.
- To sustain good customer relations.
- To maintain a constant competitive edge.

If conflict between individual executives arises then the central market-related objective(s) might be the focal point for resolving any dispute. Of course, there will always be the overriding factor of profit at the other extreme but if it is accepted that customer satisfaction is the key to longer-term stability, the temptation to over-concentrate on shorter-term resolutions will be less likely.

Defining the business

It is through the marketing approach that the nature of the business can more readily be defined along the lines of a customer orientation and this definition has far-reaching implications for the way the firm operates. The following case illustrates some of the fundamental issues that may arise from an inadequate definition of the business.

Camford Drives

Camford Drives had a workforce of a hundred or so employees and manufactured and supplied drive units for use in the chemical process industries. The company had been established for a number of years and had a reputation for good-quality products, yet it eventually suffered from foreign competition and the additional effects of a declining market. As often occurs in similar situations, the company believed strongly that it was losing out on price, but after a relatively inexpensive customer survey it became clear that there were other, more important, factors being overlooked.

Some customer dissatisfaction had set in over the years due to the company's relatively poor record of delivery and lack of attention to product design. In contrast, the survey showed that the foreign competition tended to respond more quickly and efficiently to enquiries, were able to discuss product design considerations more readily (and in English!), would often give immediate, if tentative, quotations and generally present themselves more professionally and effectively. In other words, they were achieving a higher degree of customer satisfaction even though there was a traditional customer preference for UK suppliers.

Conclusion

The company had lost considerable ground and it was obvious a reorientation was necessary if it was to continue in business. In order to adopt a customer orientation it became necessary to move away from the simple identification of manufacturing and supplying drive units and more towards the provision of 'transmission solutions' and all that this definition implied. Even as a simple philosophy this reorientation would provide the start for focusing activities on the needs of the customer and ultimately reduce the gap that previous complacency had created. There was of course, a price to pay for this reorientation but the costs of ignoring the warning signals might have been far greater, both financially and socially.

Providing future direction

While marketing acknowledges the need to focus on the customer we have also noted in the example above the need to pay attention to competitors' activity. In the broader environment in which the

Adopting a marketing orientation

business operates there are other factors at play which may affect business performance, directly or indirectly. New or improved technologies, social and cultural change, new or improved materials, variations in the economy, and developments in transport and communications. The task of monitoring these external factors is an onerous one even for the larger organizations and with a limited budget, the small business may find it virtually impossible.

However, it is clear that constantly reacting to change as it occurs or, worse, some time after it has occurred, will inevitably result in severe recovery difficulties, if not total disaster. Marketing is as much to do with looking into the future as it is with the familiar day-to-day activities of dealing with customers and their existing needs and as change is inevitable, so a preparedness to meet such change will generally increase the chances of prosperity or at the very least, survival.

Because the firm is generally dealing with future uncertainty and the cost of researching is relatively high, the small business may well choose the easier option of taking things as they come or at best, planning for the very short term. However, even working on a limited budget, certain approaches and activities are possible which will enhance the marketing capability of the small business and these will be discussed in the following chapters. At this stage it will suffice to highlight some of the dangers of taking the easier option and to demonstrate that even larger organizations can sometimes fail to act upon the longer-term, strategic influences, as the following examples illustrate:

Smiths Crisps

Back in the 1960s the Smiths Crisps company suffered heavily as a result of a failure to take account of change. Basically, the company had stuck to serving traditional outlets of pubs and smaller retail outlets from regional manufacturing and distribution bases. The advent of supermarkets and the increasing potential for crisps as a home snack (stimulated to some extent by the rapid penetration of television into households), posed a substantial threat for Smiths and the entry of Golden Wonder Crisps into the market proved to be the breaking point. The latter company, with a centralized, modern plant and bulk distribution facilities were able to service the big supermarket operations much more efficiently and, in a relatively short period, had cut Smiths' share of the market to almost half its previous size. That a well established company with market leadership should lose ground so quickly seems unthinkable, yet it seems that complacency towards identifying and acting on change was a major factor in its demise.

Acorn Computers

Acorn Computers, suppliers of the 'BBC' computer, seemed to have the national market at its feet in the early 1980s. A captive audience followed by a substantial market base in schools, colleges, and some homes might have seemed an impenetrable position, yet by the mid-1980s the company had massive debts. The rapid pace of advancement in computer hardware and software seemed to have eluded Acorn and it was eventually overtaken by those competitors who had sought to capitalize on these opportunities.

Fortunately, both of these companies eventually recovered although by different means and not without incurring a heavy penalty.

Building an image

It was stressed earlier in the text that the marketing concept has at its heart the needs of the customer and that the firm's resources should be harnessed and directed towards satisfying these needs. The image that the firm creates in the eyes of the customer is the culmination of this orientation activity yet we continuously experience situations of poor customer relations and low supplier image, suggesting that by no means is marketing as widespread, in the true sense of the word, as it should be. More often than not it is a 'people problem', exacerbated by poor management and pure ignorance of, or contempt for, the customer's needs. How many of us have personally experienced poor service and threatened never to deal with a particular supplier again? Conversely, how many businessmen have dwelt upon their own frustrations with suppliers and have then been stimulated to look inwardly at their own organizational effectiveness and overall management ability?

Adopting an effective marketing orientation involves indoctrination right down the line and this should include all employees of the firm. Education on what the firm is about, the nature of the business and above all, the focus on service to the customer is vital in creating a favourable image. A weak link in the chain, however small, represents a threat to sustaining a good reputation, for it is not just the product but the whole 'package offering' that a company makes, that creates the image.

Adopting a marketing orientation

Take for example, a customer phoning a potential supplier for the very first time with regard to a possible high-value order. An abrupt or indifferent telephone operator could easily halt any further pursuance of the enquiry and the company would be no wiser for the experience. Even if the operator had felt justified, say because of a very busy switchboard at that particular moment, it does not assist with any attempt to improve company image.

It is easy enough to cite many true-life examples of such weak links – from appalling hotel service to the ever-elusive sales manager – aside from the more common experiences of products that fail to come up to expectations and broken delivery promises. However, it is left to the reader to draw upon his or her own experiences – and a personal analysis will better underpin the marketing implications therein.

Fortunately, there are examples to which the reader can relate and where a customer orientation can almost be sensed, accepting that there may be isolated experiences to the contrary. Marks and Spencers appears to be in the authors' view, a company that is built on a reputation for customer service and through this, it has a favourable image with the public. This has come about with little or no large-scale advertising and it points to the power of word-of-mouth communication or as some would put it, the wagging tongue of the satisfied customer. The money-back guarantee policy, product quality and range, store location and layout, proficient staff and the perceived size of the organization, all contribute towards an attractive package offering in the eyes of the target audience. Such an image is unlikely to have evolved by accident for its sustenance requires a firm and positive commitment from management both to the needs of the customer and to the education, training and on-going development of the employees. Good-quality products will not make up for sloppy or indifferent staff and vice versa; nor will efficient point-of-sale service cover for poor after-sales service. The hallmark of success is attention to all of the factors which the customer perceives as a right and proper service, when contemplating parting with hard-earned cash.

At the time of writing we were constantly being told on television that British Rail were 'getting there'. Perhaps the rail-travelling reader will know whether in fact they actually have by now, but it is a good example of the considerable effort needed to reverse a previously established poor image, particularly in view of the sheer size and structure of the organization. The small, private business should take heart from this example, for being large has its own problems, particularly with regard to internal communications and control, and even more so when under public ownership.

Marketing in Small Businesses

Marketing and the selling concept

The selling concept makes the assumption that customers will be unlikely to buy the firm's products unless persuaded by heavy promotion and intense selling pressure. The focus is thus on the needs of the seller rather than the needs of the buyer, as the sole objective is to turn the goods or services offered, into income for the company.

Regrettably, such practice has tended to give sales (and marketing) a rather tarnished image, particularly where high-pressure selling has been the main inducement to buy, rather than a positive attempt to determine and service customer needs. Clearly, if the latter have been properly researched and understood then the resulting products or services should by definition require much less in the way of pressurizing techniques in order to persuade the customer to buy.

There are obvious risks in relying too heavily on the selling concept, particularly where the market may take time to develop and where the firm will be obliged to rely on repeat customer purchases. It seems that some salesmen are prepared to offer the earth to secure an order, and the various legislation pertaining to customer protection that have evolved over the years are evidence of past, dubious selling and promotional practices. Quite often it is not so much the individual salesman at fault, but rather company management who have laid down aggressive sales policies, guided only by short-term gains and in ignorance of the longer-term effects.

Newbold Kitchens

Newbold Kitchens manufactured, and marketed a range of fitted kitchens, within a region of approximately four hundred square miles. The company had around twenty employees and a turnover of £200,000 p.a. of which some £80,000 was direct to customers and the remainder through the retail trade.

In an attempt to increase direct sales the company employed Jack Symes, a former insurance salesman, to call on potential customers (those who had visited the showroom previously) in order to 'close orders'. Harold Jackson the Managing Director had commented: 'Selling is a weak spot in the company and we need someone experienced in aggressive selling – our designers are good at presentation but poor at closing the order.'

Within six months the direct orders had increased by some 20 per cent and Jack Symes was well ahead of his original target. However, customer complaints were on the increase largely as a result of broken delivery promises and differences over final costings. Conflict between Jack Symes and the designers had also arisen as the latter were taking the brunt of the complaints. By the end of the year Harold Jackson seemed to be spending most of his time visiting and reassuring dissatisfied customers and when he tackled Jack Symes the latter commented: 'I'm doing exactly what you hired me to do – sure, you have to divert the customer from the "small print" now and again but that's the name of the game in this job.'

Conclusion

Clearly Jack Symes was convinced he was doing the right thing in spite of the resort to the odd white lie. Selling an insurance policy on the same lines would probably have less repercussions and certainly it would probably be a much longer time before any problems of small print arose. As it happened in this case, word-of-mouth effect eventually took hold and visitors to the showrooms began to fall off with the result that eventually direct sales fell well below their original level.

The cost factor

In the following chapters, the various aspects of marketing are looked at in more detail, this chapter having developed only a basic framework of the essentials of the marketing concept. The fundamental considerations are the needs, wants and values of the customer and the firm's position relative to competition. There is little or no cost to any business in deliberating upon these aspects and it is not difficult to grasp that providing a greater degree of customer satisfaction than that offered by competitors has profitability implications for the individual firm. The small business in particular has the difficult task of deciding whether it can afford to adopt such a concept in view of cost implications. Similarly, it is also necessary to deliberate on the risks of not applying the concept and in the end it may have to be a trade-off decision.

Clearly, it is a question of the individual company judging the situation and deciding just what degree of uncertainty it is able to live with. If there is a strong conviction that customer needs and wants are more understood than say, competitors' activities then scarce resources may be allocated to clarify the latter. If competition is limited and customers are widespread or indeed remote from the firm due, say, to the involvement of middlemen, then the converse may apply. Whatever the situation, the adoption of a marketing profile will in itself increase the realization that the firm is indeed operating in an

Marketing in Small Businesses

uncertain environment and that there is a cost factor involved if this uncertainty is to be reduced. In the following case this realization, although leading only to marginal improvement in business, was brought about with minimal cost.

Cum-fee Beds

Jack Smith and Harry Bedford had worked for a number of years for a northern-based medium-sized manufacturer of beds. Having been made redundant due to the winding up of the company in 1982, the pair decided to form a partnership and go into business on their own.

Their strengths were mainly in production, but they felt they knew enough about the business, having some knowledge of, and contact with, suppliers and the odd distributor.

In the initial stages of setting up the company, they had obtained the usual borrowings from the bank, secured on both of their houses, and by 1985 they were turning out a range of bed sizes, including bunk beds. At this time, they found themselves stretched in production due to rather old fashioned methods and equipment. After failing to get further unsecured finance, Jack Smith had to take out a second mortgage in order to purchase more up-to-date wood-cutting and fabric-taping machinery.

As the order rate stepped up they found their existing transport inadequate and further help was needed, by 1986, for the purchase of a bigger van. Having now little security to offer, the company applied to the local authority development corporation for assistance. In making the usual formal application, the company had sought professional help to produce a monthly cash flow and they had properly costed the transport requirements. However the development corporation was concerned about the lack of supporting information on which to assess the future viability of the company and suggested that the company should seek professional marketing advice and put them in touch with an appropriate advisor. During an interview with the firm the advisor uncovered the following facts:

- The company identified its major customers as ten local outlets one of which took some 80 per cent of production and was based some twenty-three miles south of the company. On occasions, the company would take on one-off specials and was always ready to tackle this type of job.
- They had just started selling direct from the factory and had recently carried out a direct mailshot in the immediate

Adopting a marketing orientation

locality, the major theme announcing beds at *low, low prices*.
- The company was seriously considering the manufacture of convertible bed/sofas and the major distributor had given a verbal intention of taking all they could produce. They had considered delivery as far as London where a contact had suggested their product would sell with little difficulty.
- The company believed that there were no 'serious competitors' in the area, although even a search in *Yellow Pages* identified at least four other apparently similar manufacturers in the locality.
- Beyond the immediate customers (its distributors) the company had little or no information on the end-user market.
- The company identified its business as the 'manufacture of a range of single, three-quarter and double-sized beds, the occasional special one-off, and bunk beds.'

Prior to the interview, the advisor had referred to a report – lodged in a local college library – on the bed and mattress market. Although this had been produced in 1985 and represented information on market conditions in 1984, the following extracts were noted:

- Mature (i.e. little or no growth) market for the general run of beds by 1986.
- Some shift towards convertible, up-market type products, e.g. bed/sofas.
- Main reasons for buying beds: moving house and conversions to property.
- Selection will become fashion-conscious to some extent in the future.
- Tendency for smaller rooms in newly built properties.

Conclusion

It was clear that the company regarded its distributors as the main customers and thus saw little need to address the end-user market. The definition of the business as a 'manufacturer of a range of single, three-quarter and double-sized beds' is product-, rather than market-orientated and as such this might well cause some problem in the foreseeable future. For example:

- One-off specials hampering the more profitable batch production runs.
- Clash of identity between the image of low-price, direct-to-the public products and future plans for up-market

Marketing in Small Businesses

convertibles (incompatible image!).
- The ignoring of possible customer benefits such as space-saving (convertibles and in-built drawers) factors, thus missing the opportunity to enhance promotional activity, particularly for the new home buyer market (e.g. tendency for small rooms).

The statement of 'no competition' in the area was based on an assumption that no other manufacturer made exactly the same products at the same prices. Whilst this may have been true it ignored the fact that customers would normally search out and evaluate several alternative offerings before purchasing.

There was clearly an overall lack of knowledge of the end-user market and also heavy reliance on a single distributor (80 per cent of the business). The company had little idea of the type of customer buying its products or the potential for increasing market penetration through the distribution outlets.

It was finally agreed that there was generally a lack of direction and poorly planned future development. The partners eventually accepted that they needed to sit down and decide exactly what the business should be about and where they should be going in the future.

The firm had tossed a few definitions around within the context of perceived customer needs such as quality, space-saving, comfort, fashionable, and had at least acknowledged that they had started to think in terms of a customer orientation.

Although the company's application for financial support was eventually turned down by the development corporation, they had benefited to some extent, from discussions with the advisor.

As a preliminary measure they took steps to redesign all promotional literature to highlight the key customer benefits and to avoid confusion with the price–quality relationships (e.g. use of the term 'competitive' instead of 'low, low', prices).

Although the above case shows a step in the right direction, the measures taken by the company may be regarded as little more than cosmetic. For the major marketing decisions such as new product and/or new market development, the planning process requires a much greater understanding of the market forces at play.

Case study: Donprint[1]

A few months ago Donprint, a company which produces label systems

Adopting a marketing orientation

Left, Des Donohoe; right, IBM representative. Reproduced by kind permission of Tempest P.R., East Kilbride

Marketing in Small Businesses

at East Kilbride in Scotland, set out to recruit ten new employees. It wanted sales staff, people with secretarial skills, and others with printing experience. But, after advertising in local newspapers, using two recruitment agencies, scanning job centres and widening the search to cover the entire Glasgow area, the company failed to find anyone who had the required skills combined with the sense of motivation it wanted. 'It was painful,' says Desmond Donohoe, the company's sole shareholder and managing director. 'We wanted people who sought a career. The people who came to us only seemed to want a job.'

Donprint, however, refused to accept second-best. It decided to hire six people fresh from school or college and give them a six month in-house training course, covering all aspects of the business from printing to accounts, and involving a two-day induction session with the managing director himself. At the end of the course Donprint intends to assign the trainees to whatever section of the business they have shown the most aptitude for. Over the next two years it will run further courses for recruits every six months.

Donprint's attitude to training might appear remarkable even in a medium-sized company. But Donprint only has thirty-three employees, including the six trainees, and last year it only had about twenty. Though its annual sales have risen quickly, this year they are expected to reach only £1.6m. For Donprint is a company with big long-term objectives.

Donprint provides systems for printing highly durable self-adhesive labels, such as those found on personal computers or power tools. It is one of the first companies in Britain to exploit printing and computer software technology that enables companies to print part or all of their own product labels on metallized polyester, a technique which is gradually replacing the traditional anodized aluminium labels on which serial numbers have to be hammered.

Donprint is interested only in the high-quality segment of the labels market – durable labels for such industries as electronics, aerospace, defence, and appliances. It supplies its customers, which include IBM and Digital Equipment, with pre-printed labels containing standard information on the product and the keyboards, screens, and printers with which customers can compose and print variable information – such as serial numbers – on to the label. In a recent innovation, customers can now print the entire label themselves. Donprint supplies the partially printed or blank labels, and provides maintenance under a service agreement. Donprint is in competition with about twenty-five or thirty other companies in Britain, many of them US-owned, providing computerized label systems.

Donohoe, who is now thirty-seven, founded it from nothing in 1979

Adopting a marketing orientation

as a one-man business which in its first year had sales of around £20,000. Donohoe, a marine engineer by profession, had earlier worked for a multinational company that makes electro-mechanical label-making machinery. He decided that the future lay in supplying label-making systems and providing a service rather than making machinery. Donohoe now believes the total UK label market is worth about £160 million. Of this the high-technology segment for which it is aiming may be worth between £20 million and £25 million. Donohoe believes it has about 7 per cent of this segment, but his aim is to reach 20 per cent by 1990, by which time he expects sales to reach £5 million. Then he intends to turn to overseas markets.

Donohoe, a friendly but very determined Glaswegian whose father was an Irish immigrant, attributes the company's success so far partly to a determined approach to marketing and partly to high levels of efficiency: 'It's a question of looking at opportunities in the market place and being able to service them profitably on a long-term basis,' he says. The company, he says, has made profits every year since it began. His own speciality is marketing – which he studied in Glasgow – and the day-to-day running of the company is in the hands of Ray Kirk, the general manager, with whom he shares a small office.

Five years ago, after a year of persuasion, IBM approved Donprint as one of its labelling system vendors to its personal computer plant at Greenock. Both for 1985 and 1986 Donprint won one of the awards IBM gives its vendors for quality excellence. 'That entails,' says Donohoe, 'shipping a zero-defect product for twelve months – meeting their standards on all four categories: quality, delivery, administration, and response.' Donprint was also co-winner of the National Small Business Efficiency Award last year.

Efficiency, in Donohoe's view, means being able to respond quickly to customers' needs. For example, when a customer has a problem with his labelling system he connects his equipment via the telephone to Donprint's plant where any fault in the software can be diagnosed. If the fault is in the printer Donprint sends a replacement printer to the customer within twenty-four hours. Donohoe believes that a new software system the company is shortly to start marketing will leapfrog its competitors. He has also strengthened the company's prospects by gaining, at the cost of about £60,000, approval from both US and Canadian standards authorities for almost its entire range of products. These countries set very exacting standards because labels on, for example, electrical goods, have an important safety function. Donohoe sees gaining these approvals as a 'Japanese-style' long-term step. Donprint does not currently export its products or systems. But with the North American approvals customers know that products carrying Donprint labels can in effect be exported worldwide, and the

Marketing in Small Businesses

company gains credibility through having achieved the standards.

Donprint's recruiting and training policy shows the same attitude to building up long-term strengths: 'We'd much rather it could be done outside the company,' says Donohoe, 'but we want a highly able, flexible labour force.' He admits he is taking a risk because the trainees are under no obligation to stay with the company, but, he says: 'If we can't hold good people there must be something wrong with the company.'

In addition to the trainees, Donprint will also be recruiting middle-management staff to give the company 'all the disciplines it needs' to seek a USM or stock exchange listing when its current objectives are fulfilled by 1990 or 1991. 'I'm not saying we will necessarily do that,' says Donohoe, 'but if we did it would be to finance expansion abroad.' Donohoe is already pondering whether expansion would be through franchising, joint ventures or subsidiaries.

Points for deliberation

- What is the nature of Donprint's business?
- What key customer needs has Des Donohoe identified?
- To what extent is Donprint responding to these needs?
- What is Donprint's current share of the market and what are the prospects for increasing this share in the future?
- What factors point to Donprint's 'strategic view' of business?

Notes

1 *Financial Times*, 18 July 1987 (reproduced by kind permission of Financial Times Ltd).

Further reading

Cannon, T. (1986) *Basic Marketing, Principles and Practice*, 2nd edn, Eastbourne: Holt, Rinehart, and Winston.

Chisnall, P. (1987) *Small Firms in Action – Case Histories in Entrepreneurship*, Maidenhead: McGraw-Hill.

Waterworth, D. (1987) *Marketing for the Small Business*, Macmillan.

3 Understanding the marketing environment

Synopsis

The marketing environment comprises those elements, organizations, and individuals that have an influence, large or small, on the firm's business. For example, the state of the economy, the behaviour of customers, the actions of competitors, imposition of government regulations, the rate of technological development, power of suppliers and distributors, and the attitudes of the general public (see Figure 3.1).

Even the most resourceful of companies would find it difficult to pinpoint the exact nature of these influencing factors, especially as they constantly undergo change. However, a failure to understand, or take heed of, such change will generally result in the firm having constantly to react to change some time after the event; often with difficulty and, occasionally, failing to recover altogether.

For the small business, understanding these forces and anticipating environmental change may command what appears to be an unnecessarily high degree of effort and a diversion of scarce resources. However, it should not be beyond the firm to recognize and pay attention to the more influential and sensitive factors, given a reasonable grasp of the basic principles involved.

Impact of competition

There is often a danger in viewing competition too narrowly, particularly when the firm feels it has something special and unique to offer potential customers. In this situation it is common to assume that competition is very limited, or non-existent. Perhaps a good (but unfortunate) example is the Sinclair C5 electric vehicle which came to the UK market in 1983. It could strictly have been said that no direct competing product existed at that time, i.e. there was no similar three-wheeled, battery-operated enclosed vehicle which could be driven on public roads.

Marketing in Small Businesses

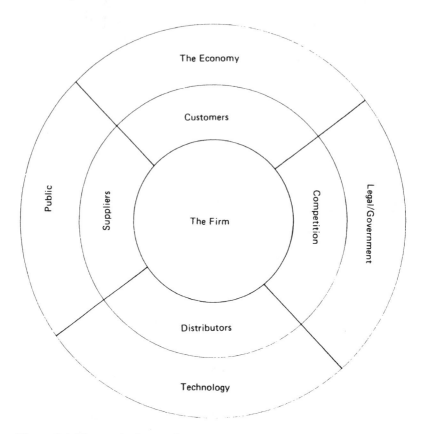

Figure 3.1 The marketing environment

However, within the broad definition of transportation the systems competing were, and still are, vast. Private cars, buses, bicycles, motorcycles, trains, and even walking, are all perfectly feasible and well-tried ways of getting from one point to another, and although the C5 was almost certainly not intended to appeal to all of these systems users, it might have been expected that those making regular, short road journeys would have been potential targets. As it happened, the existing forms of transport were obviously considered to be the more desirable, in spite of what was, at the time, considered to be the emergence of a technological innovation.

The changing nature of competition

For the small company entrenched in the confines of a local or regional market, the uncertainty of environmental changes may seem less of a threat and it is not uncommon for complacency to set in.

Carter and Simpson

Ian Carter and Mark Simpson set up a bespoke tailoring business in a northern industrial town during the late 1800s. The business had thrived for almost 80 years with two sizeable retail outlets supporting the various family generations over the years. Although there were several similar operations in the town most of these had ceased trading by the late 1950s and all but two remained by the late 1970s.

The firm had traditionally supplied a high-quality made-to-measure service and their clients mainly comprised middle- to upper-class professional males. The retail outlets also carried high-quality branded goods such as overcoats, shirts, ties, hats and gloves. Although in the first seventy years or so of trading the age range of its customers was quite wide, form 16 years to 65 years plus, by the late 1960s this was compressed to the 40 to 65 years range. By the late 1970s the company's level of business was insufficient to keep it going and the one remaining shop was closed.

Mark Simpson's great-grandson had commented:

> 'We tried to keep the business going on traditional quality lines. As we continued to remain loyal to the founders I suppose we expected the same loyalties from the families of our customers over the years. We certainly must have seen the high-street changes taking place, but perhaps it never occurred to anyone in the firm that these were a serious challenge to our traditional custom.
>
> The two other family-owned businesses in the town seem to be thriving and yet their pricing and quality didn't seem to be much different from ours. I suppose they were, and still are, somewhat more fashion-conscious but then we considered our strength to be the conservative approach to styling, so we didn't really see them as exactly competing with us.'

Conclusion

While it may seem unusual that such slow and gradual change in market conditions could be ignored to the detriment of the business, the bonds of tradition can be quite powerful. The earlier loss of the younger customer group should have been a clear

Marketing in Small Businesses

signal for change. However, even in the later years, a review of the business against competition might well have brought home the general lack of appeal of the firm's product range, as traditional conservatism gave way to more fashionable styling among the older customer groups.

Analysing competition

While it is important to recognize the existence of competition and to identify significant competitors, the knowledge will be of little use unless the firm understands what sort of presence each competitor has in the market place. This requires an understanding of the strengths and weaknesses of competing firms so that comparisons can be made. However, such comparisons should be made on the basis of a correct identification of customer needs and wants rather than solely on a firm-by-firm evaluation. In this way the firm is able to compare its position in the market with that of its market rivals and if necessary, correct any deficiencies to its advantage. Table 3.1 represents a simple analysis of supplier positionings arising from a customer survey.

Table 3.1 Competitor analysis

Competing firms	CUSTOMERS' ORDER OF NEEDS			
	1st *availability*	2nd *reliability*	3rd *price*	4th *product range*
	CUSTOMERS' PERCEPTION OF SUPPLIERS			
	Availability	Reliability	Price	Product range
Our company	weak	very strong	very strong	very weak
Competitor A	very weak	strong	average	very strong
Competitor B	strong	weak	average	weak
Competitor C	average	strong	strong	average

A sample of customers have been asked to rank their needs in order of priority and on aggregate the order of availability, reliability, price, and product range emerges. Additionally, customers have been questioned regarding the company's own standing with respect to these needs and also that of three major rivals. The aggregate finding of these perceptions shows how each company is positioned in the market and allows the firm to compare its relative position. If the company is fortunate enough to obtain estimates on competitors' market shares, this additional information can be used to further check

Understanding the marketing environment

the accuracy of customers' perceptions, assuming that the strongest supplier overall is actually enjoying the highest market share. Clearly, an ideal profile would be one of maximum strength in all categories, but this is generally difficult to achieve. However, the comparisons show where the company can improve its positioning and, in this case, improvement in availability may be possible given some acceptable increase in price, the latter being at a lower priority.

Understanding customers

An understanding of the habits, motives and influences surrounding purchasing decisions will generally help the marketer to plan and execute the marketing mix more effectively. Without this knowledge it is often difficult to judge whether, for example, the emphasis should be placed on making the price more attractive, on stressing the product quality or on constant advertising. Even though it may be desirable to give full attention to all these factors, limited resources will generally force a trade-off between them and achieving the right balance will require some understanding of the buyer's preferences, order of priorities, and sources of influence.

In consumer goods markets, where the purchase may be for personal or family use, buying behaviour is relatively complex and although well researched, it is not completely understood. In industrial markets, where the purchase is for use by the buying organization, the process is probably more readily understood, but it is by no means uncomplex in nature. Under such conditions it is difficult to generalize, and even a simplified description of the subject is probably misleading. However, it is possible to stress some of the more important issues without necessarily undermining the work of the many behavioural scientists and marketing academics who have contributed so ably to the theory.

Buying behaviour of industrial customers

It is important to recognize that in selling to other firms (as opposed to consumers) the supplier often has to consider the different needs of those individuals who may influence the buying process, as the following case describes.

Information Processing Systems

Northern area sales representative Catherine Speed explained to her sales manager, Alan Smith:

Marketing in Small Businesses

'This is the tenth time I've visited the company in as many weeks. Barry Oldham, the data processing manager, is very much on our side. He thinks our main competitor is too inflexible and that our customized approach fits their needs exactly. Yesterday he introduced me to the buyer but in spite of all the arguments about our better specification and delivery, the buyer just kept pressing for discount commitments.'

Alan:

'You did the right thing not committing us at this stage. As a matter of interest, how did our demonstration last week go down?'

Catherine:

'The data preparation supervisor apparently made some complaint about the brightness level of the screen. She said it would probably cause eye strain and the operators might refuse to handle the equipment. I did have a word with her and assured her that the colour was adjustable to an acceptable level, but the buyer seemed to be aware of this problem and he used it as a lever to negotiate prices.'

Alan:

'Don't worry too much. You've done very well seeing it's your first major potential sale. The company's engineers seem to be satisfied with the spares and servicing arrangements and I reckon we could reach a compromise on discounts. Say 5 per cent on £35,000 or 10 per cent if they opt for the £50,000 system.'

Catherine:

'Just one other thing. I forgot to mention, I'm told the company's managing director is keen on our competitor's equipment. Apparently, a colleague at the local golf club has installed one of their systems and he swears by it.'

Conclusion

It is clear that the number of individuals involved and their degree of influence in the buying process complicates the selling process. The different needs and motivations make it

Understanding the marketing environment

difficult for the marketer to concentrate upon a single unique selling proposition (USP) which can satisfy all of the individuals involved. While the buyer was looking to get the most cost-effective deal for the company, the data preparation supervisor was more concerned about the reaction from her operators, the company engineer judged maintainability as a key factor, and the managing director seemed more influenced by the opinions of his 'leisure' social group.

Consumer buying behaviour

In serving consumer markets, it is important to recognize the process through which the buyer passes when considering and ultimately making a purchase, particularly if the product has a relatively high price. In the following example the purchaser of a second-hand sports car relates his thoughts and experiences.

Stage 1

'I finally decided on a change when the tax and insurance were due. Some weeks before I'd taken a new date out to a fairly expensive restaurant and parking my old car among the expensive Jags and Granadas did nothing for my image.'

Stage 2

'I spent a couple of weeks looking through the local newspaper ads and going round various garage forecourts. I had an upper price limit in mind but at one dealer's place I saw this sports car which was £500 more than the limit. I managed to get a copy of a motoring magazine which had done a road test report on the car and this convinced me that I should buy. It was only when I was discussing it with some friends, that I heard the odd bad comment and I started to have doubts.'

Stage 3

'I went back to the dealer and he eventually reassured me that the problems had only been with earlier models of the car. The same night I must have spent a couple of hours deciding on whether I should opt for a cheaper car, but I kept imagining myself driving this sleek vehicle.'

Stage 4

'At the weekend I went back to the dealer and had another test drive. As we were driving round he explained the guarantee facilities and the 'no-fuss' financing arrangements. It felt good to see the attention the car was getting from people in the street. As soon as we got back, I signed on the spot.'

Stage 5

'In the six months that I've had the car I can't say that my social life has improved much. In fact I was feeling a bit low until I saw this advertisement about an owner's club. Members receive a regular newsletter and meet twice a year. I'm looking forward to joining. Mind you, I'm paying more insurance now and I sometimes think of the money I could have saved had I opted for the cheaper vehicle.'

These five stages of development describe several distinct phases through which the buyer passes in the purchasing process.

Initially a need is identified. In the above case, this need is largely stimulated by the experience of parking at the restaurant (external) and the desire for status (internal), e.g. the need to impress his new date.

In the second phase the buyer goes through the process of gathering information from various sources. Generally, the more expensive (relative) the product, the longer the search process will take and usually, several sources will be tapped. In this case, newspapers, visits to dealers, and friends.

Before a decision is reached the information is evaluated and at this stage, the buyer compares alternative buys in the light of his or her particular needs. The influences are made up of economic factors (what the buyer can afford), psychological factors (relative to personal motives, beliefs and attitudes) and social factors (influence of family, friends and other contact groups). In this case, our buyer is seen to be pulled between the attraction of a cheaper vehicle and the status advantage of the more expensive sports car. Note also that the road-test report (opinion leader) is a powerful influence.

Before the point of purchasing action the buyer, having gone through the various evaluations, makes the intention to purchase. However, there is generally still some perceived risk in the mind of the buyer, as the various influencing factors will be present. Here, the test drive and the reassurances from the dealer finally reduced the buyer's anxieties to the point of reaching a decision.

At the post-purchase stage, the buyer's feelings about the product may be altered according to the extent his or her needs are satisfied, through the experience of using (or consuming) the product. In the case of our buyer, the product did not appear to have come up to expectations and a tendency to think back on possible alternative buys

Understanding the marketing environment

will generally enhance these negative feelings. Also, the buyer may look to other avenues in an attempt to justify the purchase and in the case of our buyer, the car-club is seen as an opportunity for achieving group (social) identity and approval.

Market segmentation

An understanding of the above behaviour can help the marketer in a number of ways, not least in improving communications with potential buyers and existing customers (this is followed up in more detail in Chapter 8). Buying habits and behaviours are also useful for classifying customers into like-groupings, such that marketing strategy can be individually tailored to suit the more potentially profitable group or groups.

The advantages of segmenting the market in this way can best be appreciated by considering the other extreme of trying to reach too wide an audience, on the false assumption that all potential buyers of the product or service will react in much the same way. In the following case, three distinct segments show up in what might have been regarded as a single market.

Computer and Office Products Ltd (COP)

In 1987 COP decided to expand into the education sector, after some three years marketing its range of products to industry. The company considered a key strength to be on the maintenance side, as many of its small-business customers had come to appreciate the quick turnaround in repairing breakdowns. A chance contact with an independent school led to a small order and management were convinced that they could tap the wider market.

Some weeks following an extensive mailshot to local educational authority schools and colleges in the region, managing director Andy Rawes commented:

> 'The response hasn't been too good and I just wonder whether we've reached the right decision makers. We've had one or two replies from headmasters and a college computer manager asking for more information, but nothing really positive.'

Salesman, Simon Brown, attempted to explain the situation:

> 'The major college in the region carries its own maintenance facilities and the central computing purchasing unit seems to act on requests from individual departments within the college. I can't see that stressing maintenance facilities will

43

carry much weight for this customer. Local schools in the region act through central purchasing authorities so contacting individual headmasters isn't likely to stimulate much interest. In any event, educational establishments, as I've found out, expect a discount so we'll have to revise our pricing policy.'

Conclusion

It is evident that not only is the education sector somewhat different from the business sector in which the company was currently dealing but also, differences in buying habits occur within the education sector itself. There are at least three different market segments identifiable which require some variation of the marketing mix and for one segment at least, the company's key strength in maintenance seems a non-starter. The cost of tailoring the marketing mix to each segment may well be prohibitive, while on the other hand, attempting to reach all potential users with a standard approach, is unlikely to attract universal appeal.

In the end, it is a matter of judging the most attractive segment(s) that the firm is able to serve, without overstretching its resources.

Technology

The impact of technological change on the firm is very much industry-dependent. For example, while developments in computer technology have led to many small businesses entering that industry, the rate of change of technology has also been responsible for the collapse of many companies who could not afford to keep up with the changes.

Rapid product obsolescence and the adoption of new manufacturing processes sometimes make it difficult for the small business to compete effectively and it often becomes necessary to find a niche in the market where competition is minimal. For example, engineering companies possessing modern machining technology geared up to the mass production of precision components, would be unlikely to pursue customers requiring one-off specials or very small batch orders and therefore the smaller company, stuck with the older machining technology, may find it more profitable to seek out these opportunities, than trying to compete head-on:

Managing director: Field Engineering Ltd: 'We managed to come through the recession by the skin of our teeth. Some local firms had gone to the ground and others had diversified into new

Understanding the marketing environment

areas requiring investment in up-to-date manufacturing technology.

'There was no way we could have afforded new machines and for a time, we had to deal with excessive price cutting. Eventually we had to decide whether to wind up the business or seek new markets.

'Fortunately, and by chance, my co-director recognized a gap in the textile machinery maintenance market. With the slight up-turn in the industry and the general slim-down of in-house maintenance staff resulting from the recession, the opportunities for maintenance sub-contracting seem to be growing.

'We now have the expertise to strip down and repair fairly complex machinery and supply replacement, engineered components. It's nothing like our original business but at least we've survived and we are now aware that things don't stand still in this industry.

'Of course, there are other firms in the business and it's just a matter of maintaining an acceptable level of quality and delivery to keep a viable share of the market. We do realize that for the longer term we will need to tap other markets and that we have to *plan now*, rather than waiting for change to arrive before we act.'

In many situations it is difficult, if not impossible, to stay with old technologies and the firm has to decide whether or not it can cope with the risks and financial investment involved. Dealing with uncertainty is, of course, part of everyday business life. However, the decision to adopt new technology as a means to developing new products or improving existing products, probably represents the greatest area of uncertainty for the small manufacturing business. Not only is there a danger of over-optimism regarding the successful outcome of technical developments, but also the lack of a proper assessment of the financial and market implications will almost certainly compound the problem.

Managing director: medical equipment company: 'The concept behind the development was both to provide a home-based self-treatment system for patients and a truly portable machine. Many patients just cannot go away for holidays like most of us, because of the need for regular hospital treatment.

'Reliability and accuracy are absolutely vital for the system and so we felt the need to adopt the new microprocessor technology. We ploughed our own savings into the development, borrowed on the strength of our personal assets and the building, and took advantage of a government grant. After three years, the development had also used up a large slice of the profits from the traditional side of the business, but the prototype machine was still incomplete.

'When we thought success was just round the corner, another technical snag would arise and, in the process of establishing contacts in the National Health Service, we also realized just how badly we had misunderstood the marketing side. While most end-user patients would see the system as a real breakthrough, NHS funding opportunity seemed to be deteriorating by the year. Of course, a few well-off patients could afford to buy a machine, but the majority would, I'm sure, have to rely on some sort of government grant.

'After three-and-a-half years the technical problems have now been solved and we have two working prototypes, but the biggest problem is yet to come. Looking back I think I was prepared to blame anyone but myself for the slow progress and the frustration. Given a similar situation in the future, I would definitely look much more thoroughly at the market and certainly consider alternative ways of financing the development. It is difficult to plan with any degree of accuracy under the circumstances, but at least it will pay to sit down and think through the issues, as opposed to gambling on a purely personal idea.'

Conclusion

The case really speaks for itself and the latter comments of the managing director sum up the problem quite adequately. In fairness, the managing director had identified a prominent gap in the market and, with such a socially acceptable product, few would entirely agree with his own self-criticisms and in particular, his final comment. Although regrettable in this case, over-optimism in coping with new technology and insufficient market awareness were the key underlying causes. It is quite feasible that the development could have been financed better, but often financial problems occur as a result of mismanagement in other areas. Grasping technological opportunity is admirable in itself, but it should be accompanied by a careful assessment of the possible long-term impact on the business, given the inherent uncertainties.

Suppliers, resellers, and distributors

The structures of markets have considerable impact on the bargaining powers of the members and the way in which they compete.

The marketing chains, through which raw materials and goods pass on their way to a given end-user market, are quite complex for some industries. In Figure 3.2, which is probably only a simplified picture of the actual events taking place, the chain starts with the extraction of basic raw materials which then pass through a number of manufacturing, stocking, and distribution processes. Within the broad definition of 'windows and/or window frames' the three different raw materials identified suggest that the frame manufacturing technologies are probably quite different (a point to note within the context of technological change discussed previously). It may also be assumed that with the gradual penetration of the newer materials (aluminium and PVC) the traditional timber supply chain (for the market concerned) would have suffered some considerable erosion of market share over the years.

On the distribution side, both the growth in the multiple DIY chains and direct-selling operation would also have attacked the smaller, traditional channels and almost certainly have affected their bargaining powers with the manufacturers, at the expense of the former. In essence, it represents a picture of constant change in which new entrants come into the market, some traditional suppliers disappear, and the fight for the market share continuously intensifies. Under such conditions the larger manufacturers may attempt to buy out suppliers or buy into distribution channels (backward or forward integration) in order to enhance and defend their market position. For the smaller company it is almost impossible to meet major competitors head-on and it becomes largely a question of finding and developing a profitable niche in the market. In addition to developing good relations with customers (or distributors) and a particular expertise, the firm may also benefit from securing strong ties with suppliers.

Metal Component Suppliers (MCS)

MCS supply a variety of well-known proprietary product manufacturers with small, metal components. The manufacturing process involves the deep-drawing of strip alloys to very high precision. The firm has developed a reputation over the years, for producing high-volume, complex components with a flexibility to adapt to changing customer requirements, quickly and effectively.

Buyer, Jack Medlock, comments:

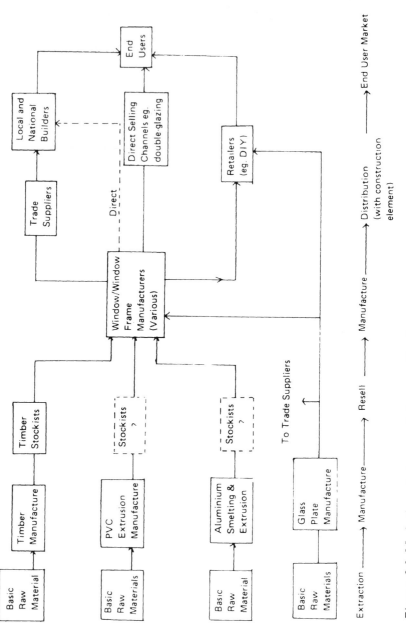

Figure 3.2 Marketing chains – windows and/or frames

Understanding the marketing environment

'We work hand-in-hand with the production and sales department. The quality of the final component is directly related to the quality of the strip metal we buy in, so close negotiation between sales, design, and manufacturing is vital.

'There are five major strip-metal suppliers on our books, each with different strengths and weaknesses and we call on these according to the problems at hand. For example, a major West German supplier can always be relied upon for accurate specification and delivery, but the company is inflexible when it comes to meeting unexpected changes in customer specification. In contrast, one of our UK based suppliers will react quickly when our customers' requirements change for one reason or another. The continuity and balance of our work enables us to maintain good relationships with all of our suppliers, gives us a good bargaining position and, of course, the end result is the satisfied customer.

'Our particular strength is in deep-drawing and we have stuck to this technology over the years, often turning down requests for less complicated, pressed components.'

Conclusion

Although MCS did not consider themselves to be marketing-oriented in the formal sense, the emphasis on customer satisfaction is a clear indication that at least, there was an informal acknowledgement of the application of the marketing concept. This is a classic example of where the harnessing of the firm's resources – in this case design, production, sales and buying – are directed towards satisfying customer needs. It should be noted that at the time of writing, the company was enjoying high profitability and had few serious competitors. The specialization in deep-drawing and the build-up of expertise and reputation in this technology had, no doubt, strengthened the firm's competitive edge – a clearly successful strategy which would account for the turning down of other, seemingly comparable business opportunities. With such a sharp business definition, close relationships with suppliers and customers, and a tightly knit operation, the firm is also in a much better position to predict, and quickly respond to changes in the environment.

Government, public, and the economy

While the firm may have some level of control over its fate within the immediate environment of customers and suppliers, it is generally at

Marketing in Small Businesses

the mercy of the wider environment comprising the legal, political, social and economic forces. With an effective monitoring system, certain changes in these forces can be predicted with relative ease, while others may occur with little warning.

In general, the firm's business will be affected to some extent by many factors, including the rate of inflation, political change, level of disposable income, interest and currency exchange rates, taxation, public attitudes, and a host of regulations governing the way in which businesses are required to be conducted and to be accountable. From a marketing perspective such forces may have an impact on: pricing (inflation); advertising and product safety standards (codes of practice, government regulations); exports and/or imports (currency exchange rates); and market growth or decline (disposable income).

The following examples serve to show the effects of some of these forces and, in particular, where realization came too late.

Carpet distributor: 'Inflation pushed up the rent and rates and the cost-price of the carpets. I had no other option but to increase the retail prices of the products. On top of this, cheaper imports from Belgium seem to be filling most other shops in the area and, in the end, I just couldn't compete.'

Provincial hotel proprietor: 'We were in a good position with the weak pound. Over the last couple of years I had built up a steady increase in the summer season trade with the growth in US visitors to the area and then the Libyan crisis hit us. I just didn't have any contingency plans and it was far too late to think of developing other possible markets, although I managed to attract some cut-price weekend trade. On the whole, we were very badly hit.'

Managing director: engineering company: 'The American agency contact seemed just what we needed to boost business. When the negotiations eventually got underway it became clear that the conditions they were demanding were just too much. Product liability insurance cover, exclusive distribution rights, stiff contractual clauses – it seemed everything was one-sided and I wondered if we had any say at all! On top of that, the product was required to conform to standards I wasn't exactly familiar with. It was just a waste of two months toing and froing.'

Director: component supplies: 'We had enjoyed a thriving business supplying a small number of manufacturers of proprietary products. I suppose we didn't think too much about

Understanding the marketing environment

the end-user markets until the orders started to run down. We eventually realized that the decline in business was somehow linked to the rise in unemployment and that the end-user markets were probably in the lower income bracket. It seems unbelievable, looking back, that we didn't see the writing on the wall earlier. We now appreciate that we need to look beyond our immediate customers and into the markets they serve.'

The emphasis the firm needs to give to environmental analysis will depend on the particular markets served and the type of products or services supplied. For example, in certain industries technological developments move relatively slowly and also some market segments are less sensitive to economic down-turns than others. In order for the firm to decide where the emphasis should be placed it must of course, have an initial understanding of the complete environment in which it operates.

Checklist

How much information does the firm currently have, about:

- The market?
- Customers and potential customers (end-users)?
- Competitors?
- Significant trends?

What information is needed?

- Market potential?
- Current share?
- End-user needs, buying habits, and trends?
- Competitors' strengths and weaknesses?
- Company/product strengths and weaknesses?

Other factors that affect the business through change:

- Technology?
- Economy?
- Suppliers?
- Distributors?

What are the sources of help and information?

Secondary data
- Government sources.

Marketing in Small Businesses

- Trade associations.
- Libraries.
- Local educational establishments.
- Chambers of commerce.
- Internal (company) information.

Primary data
- Private consultancies.
- Educational establishments operating consultancy.
- Internal company records.
- Self-help survey.

Why the need for information?

- In a better position to prepare for anticipated changes.
- Be more competitive.
- Better use of resources.
- More control.

Is it worth the time and cost?

- Depends how well the company can live with uncertainty.
- Private consultancy relatively expensive if primary data required.
- Collecting secondary data is low-cost but may be time-consuming to evaluate and interpret.
- If internal system organized, customer and product analyses are relatively easy to compile and often very useful for anticipating and acting upon change.
- A self-help survey need not be that expensive – personal interviews, by telephone or use of salesmen can elicit useful information.
- Help and advice from local chambers of commerce, or DTI (small firms assistance) or local, educational establishments (business and management studies departments) will often be provided free of charge.

Case study: Impact of house prices[1]

Escalating house prices have delighted owners but their possible effect on wages and broader price levels in the economy is a matter of growing concern for the government. Several independent economists are arguing that house price inflation might put the government's drive against inflation at risk. There are worries too about the expansion of borrowing, much of it to the personal sector, which has accompanied

Photo copyright: Huddersfield Polytechnic.

the surge in house prices, and fears that wages might be pushed to excessive levels because of sharp regional differences in house price rises.

Yet there remain broad areas of disagreement among economists about how important the various links are between house prices, wage levels, and retail price inflation. Even the Bank of England, which identified a number of possible inflationary side-effects of the house price boom in its *Quarterly Bulletin*, is cautious about drawing firm conclusions. Since 1956, the average house price in Britain has multiplied by about 18 times. The retail price index, by comparison, has increased about 8.5 times. There have been stark differences between regions. Between 1970 and 1986, house prices in London rose 9.5 times. In Wales, they rose 6.8-fold.

The upswing has been caused mainly by strong real earnings growth. That has stimulated demand in a market where long planning and building times mean the amount of housing supply available can respond only slowly.

The link between earnings and house prices is evident in the Building Societies Association's ratio of house prices to earnings which, in the post-war period, has remained consistently around 3.5 and rarely strays below two or above five. In the first quarter of 1987, the ratio stood at 3.58.

Although the BSA believes it is rising wages that push up prices, there are other factors that might have helped to prompt house price rises. It is possible that the link also works in the opposite direction. In both the early 1970s and 1980s there were significant increases in council house rents. Recently that has encouraged tenants to buy their homes, but some have also moved into the private sector.

Population movements, a higher incidence of divorces and an increasing desire among the younger generation to move out of their parents' homes have all increased the number of separate households. That trend towards one and two-person households, however, has exacerbated the mismatch between demand and a national housing stock dominated by two- or three-bedroomed family houses.

Mortgage rates rose in the late 1970s but following 1982 they fell from a high of about 15 per cent to about 11.25 per cent. The growing competition between banks and building societies to attract borrowers may also have stimulated the popularity of house buying.

The recent one-percentage-point rise in base rates has stopped mortgage rates falling further, at least for now. But house prices are thought to be relatively insensitive to small moves in interest rates and a much larger rate rise would probably be necessary to dampen sales significantly.

Understanding the marketing environment

In the south-east of England, price rises have been pushed higher by improved communications – most notably by completion of the M25 motorway. There is greater competition for land, which is frequently in limited supply because of planning restrictions.

In addition, there is an identifiable link between an area's unemployment rate and the pace of house price inflation. Higher unemployment means lower earnings and a reduced demand for houses to buy, easing the upward pressure on prices.

Those distortions and the general scale of price rises across the country is a matter of concern for the Bank of England. Its latest *Quarterly Bulletin* said they might be a factor in sustaining inflationary expectations and determining wage settlements.

The Bank of England has also questioned the prudence of the substantial expansion in credit to consumers, of which borrowing for house purchases is the largest component. Figures published by the BSA on August 22 showed the number of mortgages foreclosed by building societies at record levels, which tends to underscore such concerns.

There is a direct link between house costs, including mortgage repayments, which form part of the retail price index, and pay, in turn influenced by wage bargaining. However, there is disagreement among economists about less tenuous relationships.

Mr Tim Congdon, chief economist at Shearson Lehman Securities, believes the housing market has a profound influence on consumer behaviour. That in turn affects other variables in the economy, including wages and prices: 'Decisions about housing are absolutely basic to other spending. That is common sense,' he said.

He argues that may mean that house price rises lead to increases in inflation and wages – as well as the other way round. In other words, there is a full circle connecting increased house prices with rising retail prices and higher earnings.

Other economists give the housing market a less significant role in determining the rate of inflation. 'It would come quite low on my list of priorities,' said Mr Bill Martin, chief UK economist at stockbrokers Phillips & Drew. 'House prices are one of a number of factors but they are not the most important.'

It is an issue that is unlikely to be resolved. The difficulty is trying to identify the sequences of events connecting the various economic indicators when there are many components involved. House prices rising faster than inflation, for instance, increases the theoretical wealth of individuals. Although it is difficult to realize that gain, it may increase home owners' ability to borrow for other spending through extended mortgages.

At the same time, there is some evidence that an increasingly large chunk of money released when owners move houses is being spent in shops, increasing demand and adding to inflationary pressures.

However, it is also possible that this 'equity withdrawal' is used merely to change the composition of individuals' asset portfolios: the money realized is put into other investments such as shares or unit trusts rather than spent in the shops. The fact that the ratio of saving by consumers to income remains relatively constant supports that argument.

The buoyant housing market may be putting pressure on construction activities. The concern is that bottlenecks in the supply of labour and materials that result will also push up prices and suck in an excessive volume of imports. Regional distortions in housing costs make problems of labour mobility more acute. Recent surveys by the Confederation of British Industry and the Institute of Directors provide evidence of skilled labour shortages.

Although those are currently thought to be relatively isolated and are affecting particular regions or industrial sectors more than others, any broadening of these shortages might lead to upward pressure on wages and act as a constraint on output growth.

Points for deliberation
- What factors appear to have contributed to the demand for housing?
- What type of housing has not followed the general trend in prices?
- What factor appears to have a negative effect on house prices?
- What other environmental factors appear to be influenced by house prices?
- What types of small business activities are likely to be influenced by house prices?
- What are the problems of forecasting trends in price changes?
- To what extent do analysts agree regarding the impact of house prices?

Case study: Industrial manufacturing and marketing[2]

If there is a Cinderella in the world of marketing it must surely be industrial marketing. While more and more sectors of the British economy are waking up to the essential role of marketing in their future prosperity and growth, many industrial manufacturing companies still seem to be sleeping off the hangover of long gone days when the market was what you could make, rather than what you could sell.

Photo copyright: Huddersfield Polytechnic.

Marketing in Small Businesses

It is perhaps inevitable that different sectors of the economy should be at different stages of maturity in their approach to and their appreciation of marketing. The world of fast moving consumer goods has had to learn effective marketing approaches to respond to fierce domestic competition. Much the same is true of retailing, where most of the major high street chains now invest considerable time, effort, and money in developing the company brand in consumers' minds.

So why is industrial marketing so far behind? It, too is suffering fierce competition across virtually all its product lines. It, too, has extensive opportunities to build growth by satisfying existing and latent customer needs. Yet all the evidence suggests that the industrial manufacturing sector in general neither fully understands the markets in which it competes nor appreciates the role that effective marketing can play in generating strong, internationally competitive business.

The reasons for this state of affairs are numerous, complex and open to debate. But some of the most likely are as follows:

The structure of industrial manufacturing

Large sections of manufacturing are still dominated by small firms. Not only does their size weigh against them (big customers have less and less time to spare for a myriad of small suppliers), but such companies often cannot afford a professional marketing department. Instead, they rely upon a handful of salespeople and agents. The strategic issues of marketing are rarely, if ever, discussed by a top management that is primarily concerned with making sure the goods go out of the factory gate.

Small customer number

The FMCG companies were forced into market research and planned marketing approaches by the need to reach large numbers of consumers. Much of the industrial manufacturing sector has only a small number of customers. Not only does this bring problems of over-reliance on a few key accounts, but it encourages the view that marketing is unnecessary, 'because we already know our customers'. This narrow view is doubly dangerous. On the one hand, it fails to recognize that knowing the customer is a much more intensive and difficult task than most companies realize. On the other, it ignores the role that effective marketing plays in assessing whether the existing customers are the *right* customers.

Industrial manufacturing is a declining sector

As the industrial base declines and competition increases, margins are

Understanding the marketing environment

continually shaved. In many cases, customers are forcing suppliers to reduce prices or lose the business. (Unipart several years ago issued such an ultimatum to all its suppliers. They had little option but to agree.) Against such a background, marketing is all too often seen as an unnecessary expense. The money spent on market research, say, could buy a much-needed new machine. The issue of whether that machine is the right one for producing what the customer wants may not be given the consideration it deserves – and no one knows any better, because the data is not available.

The cost of changing the infrastructure

As capital equipment costs rise, the investment in plant becomes a major obstacle to change. Having invested, say, £500,000 in a machine only three years ago, few companies will have the courage to scrap it in order to make something different. Yet, if the market for the product has changed, then it is pointless to continue producing what can either not be sold or must be sold at reduced margins, if more profitable alternatives exist. The conflict between production orientation and marketing orientation is all too often resolved in favour of the production side.

A bird's eye view of industrial manufacturing in the UK begs the question: 'Is lack of marketing a cause or an effect of the continual decline?' Whatever the answer it is clear that marketing is an essential part of the cure. If British manufacturing industry is to drag itself out of the doldrums it must:

Define who the customer is. The immediate purchaser in industrial manufacture is often only an intermediary, assembling a variety of components to make his own product (which may itself be a sub-assembly of something else). Far too many manufacturing companies fail to look beyond the immediate client company to *its* customers. A clear understanding of the end-market can enable the supplier company to predict and react to important trends long before the immediate customer suddenly rings up wanting a new specification; it can also enable the supplier to help the customer plan responses to the market. In doing so, of course, it strengthens its special relationship.

This knowledge of the end-market has a double value. Because it is possible to demonstrate to the immediate customer that he will sell more at a higher price, the supplier, too, can demand and receive higher margins.

Really get to know customers. The one theme that emerges most strongly from the rash of books on business excellence is that the closer a company gets to its customers, the more money it is likely to make from them.

Marketing in Small Businesses

Very few British industrial companies put this theory into effect. The exceptions stand out. ICI Paints, for example, places its own technical people on the shopfloor of vehicle assembly plants. An unnecessary expense? Not if an isolated problem in paint composition can bring the whole assembly line to a halt.

Getting close to the customer pays off in a number of critical ways. First, even when the number of potential customers may be relatively stable or even growing, the international trend in manufacturing is to have fewer suppliers.

The growth of symbiotic relationships between companies is clearly the way of the future. It is now becoming entrenched in other sectors. In food retailing, for example, Bejam has forged links with suppliers such as Bowyers to develop new ranges of products to both companies' benefit. There are examples of close symbiosis in industrial manufacturing, but all too often companies take a stand-off attitude that stems from a largely irrational fear of giving away technical secrets.

Closeness to the customer creates an entry barrier for competitors. All other things being equal, customers will normally stick with the supplier they know and trust, rather than a newcomer. The tighter the relationship, the more difficult for an outsider to break in. Japanese companies work very hard at creating this kind of entry barrier – with evident success.

Get to know the competition. By and large, British manufacturers are woefully ill-informed about their competitors and particularly overseas competitors. It takes a company like JCB to demonstrate what can be done. JCB has held off much larger Japanese and American rivals by learning everything it can about their products, their plans, their strengths and weaknesses. It literally takes their products apart to understand them.

Put stress on quality. The quality movement now sweeping the US and starting to take a hold in Europe and Britain is not a fad. The Japanese proved that a passionate commitment to quality pays off dramatically. The majority of British manufacturing still operates on the theory that achieving 100 per cent consistency of product is uneconomic, that getting the last few per cent right costs more than the previous 95 per cent. In reality, however, these companies greatly underestimate both the internal costs of scrap, rework and waste of both management and employee time – and the cost of lost customers and lost markets.

The plain fact is that in almost every sector, customers are increasingly willing to pay extra for quality. Even where they are unwilling to pay for it, they still demand it. The example of Jaguar is perhaps a model of how major manufacturers are having to deal with their suppliers. When it analysed the causes of customer complaints, the car manufacturer found that 60 per cent of them were caused by component failure. It started to remedy matters by returning batches of components that were not perfect. One month it sent back 22,000.

Jaguar's suppliers are now allowed a small and decreasing margin of error. If they exceed that margin, they become liable for the costs of putting it right, no matter where in the production chain (or in service) the fault is discovered. The costs of not delivering quality have now become too high to be ignored.

The point here is that companies in other countries are far further along this path than British suppliers. Companies that cannot deliver quality will increasingly find themselves out of the running as they compete with companies that can and do. Concentrating on price is an inadequate solution. Companies that concentrate on quality have almost universally found that their costs of production and service fall too, enabling them to compete on both quality and price – a formidable combination.

Realize that manufacturing is service. Why did IBM manage so quickly to penetrate and dominate the market for personal computers? It was not the excellence of its dealer network, nor of the product itself and certainly not the price. The reason was that customers increasingly require assurance that the product they have bought will continue to function and is supported by an efficient service organization that will be available when needed. It is, if you like, another aspect of closeness to the customer. And maintaining an effective service operation provides valuable feedback that can be used to keep improving the product.

Realize that design is important. Although some observers have recently gone over the top in suggesting that the ills of British manufacturing could be cured by better design (a patent fallacy, when design is only one part of the marketing mix), the fact remains that design can create a significant marketing edge.

Improve the quality of sales. The quality of the sales effort lies largely in the quality of the sales staff. Industrial marketing is increasingly reliant on customer confidence – which can be readily undermined by salespeople who are not technically competent in the products they sell and the uses to which those products are likely to be put. There is undoubtedly an urgent need for an upgrading of the calibre and capabilities of British manufacturing sales staff in general.

There is an urgency about all these aspects of marketing, if the British manufacturing sector is to pull out of its headlong slide into obscurity. The signs are there that it can be done. In the speciality paper industry, for example, companies such as Wiggins Teape and their continental equivalents have seen off the Japanese, having first –

Marketing in Small Businesses

through plain failure to carry out competitor analyses – allowed them to gain a foothold.

In engineering, Coventry-based AE's healthy profits are in large measure a result of close attention to market planning. It supplements a detailed five-year plan for existing and potential markets with monthly reviews based on extensive market research. AE sees the fact that it has a narrow customer base of around 400 as an advantage, for it can get to know each of them individually, in detail. Many, indeed most of these customers are overseas and AE's attitude towards the export markets has lessons for less successful exporters. It values a technically competent sales person who can speak German way above a lengthy technical manual, because it knows that confidence in the company (essential when customer may have to spend up to £500,000 testing a component) results from confidence in the person at the sharp end.

There are, of course, many other examples of British manufacturing companies that are succeeding in national and international markets because they have taken marketing disciplines to heart. But what can be done about the vast majority that have still not woken up to the necessity? A major task of education remains to be done, and the institute is playing its part through the introduction of more training courses aimed specifically at the industrial manufacturing sector.

Points for deliberation

- What is the basic conflict between a 'production orientation' and a 'marketing orientation'?
- What factors of the market need to be addressed more thoroughly?
- How should companies respond, in marketing terms, to the environment?
- What future likely threats and opportunities does the UK manufacturing sector face and what are the implications for small businesses in:
  1 Manufacturing?
  2 Service industries (including distribution)?
- In what way do the industrial and fast moving goods sectors differ in their approach to marketing and why?
- Why is it considered important for the firm to look beyond its immediate clients?
- Is it feasible to define manufacturing as 'a service'?
- What changes have had a significant impact on the manufacturing sector?

Understanding the marketing environment

- What are the main benefits of 'getting to know the customer and competition'?

Notes

1 *Financial Times*, 1 September 1987 (reproduced by kind permission of Financial Times Ltd).
2 'Cinders must go to the ball', *Marketing* (editorial), 31 July 1986, 44–5 (reproduced by kind permission of Haymarket Publications Ltd).

Further reading

Levicki, C. (1984) (ed.), *Small Business Theory and Policy*, London: Croom Helm.
Clifton, P., Nguyen, H., and Nutt, S. (1985) *Marketing Analysis and Forecasting*, London: Heinemann.
Ganguly, P., Hilton, S. (1983) 'Lifespan analysis of business in the UK', *British Business*, 12 August, 838–45.
Hague, P. N. and Jackson, P. (1987) *Do Your Own Market Research*, London: Kogan Page.

4 Marketing planning

Synopsis

Marketing planning involves a conscious effort to identify and act upon market changes. The process also requires that the firm has an understanding of its 'position' in the market both with respect to its customers and intermediaries and to its competitors. With this knowledge and understanding, the firm will be in a better position to plan for change and be more able to manage resources effectively. As a highly formalized process it can be described as illustrated in Figure 4.1.

Importance of a formalized approach

Of course, such a highly formalized system will not necessarily suit every small business, for a variety of reasons. Some may find it too time-consuming or beyond their means to access and evaluate factors in the market, while others will thrive on a less formalized approach and may see no need to adopt what appears to be a rather rigid procedure. It is also the case that there are those individuals who can sense and swiftly act upon market opportunities with great success (for example, Alan Sugar, Amstrad Computers and Richard Branson, Virgin Co.) while the rest of the business community can only stand and stare. Such entrepreneurs are, however, few and far between and the average small business is rarely in a position to risk all, particularly when there are many imponderables and anxieties regarding the future of the business.

For this reason alone, any reasonably adaptable process which may go both towards reducing uncertainties and instilling some order in the way business is conducted, must be beneficial to some extent. In the final analysis, it is for the business to decide just what facets of marketing planning are feasible and whether the benefits outweigh the costs.

Marketing planning

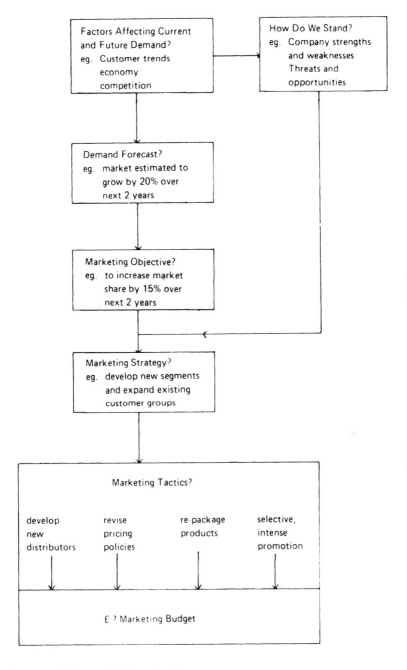

Figure 4.1 The marketing planning process

Forecasting demand

The basis of planning is first assessing what the company can realistically achieve and, from this, deciding on the means by which these aims can be met. If, as is usually the case, the company has an objective of increasing sales and profits, the more that these can be expressed in specific, quantifiable, terms the better the means can be evaluated, put into action, and monitored. If expansion of the existing product/market is required, then a simple forecast may suffice, based on current and past sales figures, with some allowance for any predicted market changes. If the plan involves some significant change in the business such as the addition of new products or the development of a new market, this obviously adds to the problems of forecasting.

In either case, it is advisable to make some attempt to deliberate on all of the factors that may have an impact on future sales, such as distributors (if appropriate), competition, economic trends, customers and the effect of price and promotional effort. The following cases demonstrate one company's approach to marketing planning.

Travelway Ltd (A)

Ronald Finlay had built up a successful travel agency business in an area which, at the time of the formation of the company (1982), seemed the least likely in view of the amount of competing agencies. By 1986 he had built up the business to five outlets (including one flight-only operation) turning over some £2 million sales and employing fifteen staff.

Commenting on the success of the business, Ronald Finlay stated:

'Although I can't say I adopted a formal planning approach in the first place, I'd be the first to admit that my marketing training, including some time in teaching the subject, had a good deal to do with my way of thinking. For example, I'd recognized the deficiencies in some of the travel agents I myself had used from time to time. I had also read up on developments in the tour industry and scanned the financial newspapers for the usual reports. This confirmed my belief that the opportunities were there and that even the economic situation would not adversely affect those customer groups who regularly holiday abroad.

'I felt that I knew what the customer wanted. In essence, it was a *service*. Whether it was a rail ticket to London or a holiday in the Bahamas, patience, advice, reassurance, and basic politeness was part of the package sought by customers.

Marketing planning

'By the time I was ready to launch the first agency I had a rough idea of how much share of the local market (based on population statistics) I could build up. Of course, I realized that I would need to advertise and pay for the opening promotional campaign. Concentrating on all of these factors greatly helped to produce a sound business plan and the appropriate cash flows and, of course, I needed all the support I could get in order to convince the bank manager.

'I suppose it could have gone the other way, but I must have had the gods on my side.'

Conclusion

Luck, of course, is always a factor, but there is plenty of evidence to show that Ronald Finlay thought through the important issues.

For example, customer potential and needs, competition weaknesses, impact of the economy, market trends, and marketing effort needed had, collectively, contributed to the credibility of the sales forecast. As it happened, Travelway's expansion plans were accompanied by the same deliberation. For example, a recognition of the growth in overseas self-catering holidays was a key factor in the decision to open the flight-only operation and geographical location of the newer agencies was always preceded by a careful search of both the local population distribution and the competition.

Setting marketing objectives

If market data is readily available, it is useful to attempt to set marketing objectives in terms of market share, rather than setting some arbitrary sales figure. In this way, the measurement of achievmment is much more meaningful for it is an indication of how well or badly the firm is doing with respect to changes in the market.

Travelway Ltd (B)

'Just think,' said Ronald Finlay, 'In 1987 the tour operators will probably handle some eight million package holidays. Even at a modest £200 per holiday that represents a market value of some £1.6 billion, and as my tour sales alone are likely to hit the £1 million mark, this will be about 0.06 per cent of the total market. Even if I just hang on to this share, the business will grow because the market is actually growing. Of course, there is

Marketing in Small Businesses

nothing I can do about price setting and my commission is fixed at a constant level, but I aim to increase my market share by concentrating on promotion.

Deciding on the optimum strategy

In planning for growth (or survival) the options, in basic terms, are somewhat limited. It may be a question of getting more out of the current market, launching new or modified products, nurturing new markets, or even venturing into completely new product/market areas. The last option obviously has its problems and justifiably so: the firm should explore the more readily adaptable moves before diversifying away from the existing business, unless the opportunity is too good to pass up.

Travelway Ltd (C)

Ronald Finlay had faced the real possibility of growth limitations in 1984. He had had to cope with the problem of deciding between trying to stimulate more business within the existing agencies or setting up new shops in other areas of the region. The latter obviously had greater cost implications, but he could never be absolutely sure that he had exploited all of the opportunities within his existing operations:

'My agencies in the main, dealt with family bookings. From personal experience, I knew that local clubs, from time to time, arranged trips for their members such as for sporting occasions or purely for relaxation. I also recognized that the firm could benefit from more exposure through sponsorship, such as identification with local football teams. For the cost of twenty-two or so football strips, the company name would have a constant exposure, although to a limited audience.'

Benefits of going for market share

For many businesses, increasing market share will generally bring additional benefits, leading to opportunities for greater profitability. Establishing some sort of leadership or reputation even in a small, but special niche of the market, can give the firm advantages which competitors might find difficult to match.

Travelway Ltd (D)

Over the period 1984 to 1986, Ronald Finlay had consciously planned to increase market share on the package tour side of the business. He had come to the conclusion that he would take on some 10 per cent more than the current market growth would provide with little or no increase in staff. However, this would involve installing new technology in the form of computerized, on-line, booking and enquiry facility, but he estimated that the cost would be recovered in a short period of time, should he achieve his objective.

Rather than promote the full range of package holidays, Ronald Finlay decided to push the offers of one major operator, which he did by advertising in the local newspaper and by shop-window displays.

'In 1986, I achieved the highest sales for 'operator x' among all agencies in the region,' Finlay commented. 'Apart from winning a free trip to the States, I not only had improved my bargaining power with operator x but I had representatives of a rival operator calling more frequently than usual. Aside from all this, the extra (free) publicity was probably far more beneficial than any paid advertising campaign.

'Of course, all businesses need that element of luck, but you can never know just how much it may be responsible for success. What I do know is that without a conscious, planned effort, luck wouldn't have been enough on its own.'

Exercising controls

The frequency with which plans are reviewed will depend to a large extent on how quickly market changes take place and/or the confidence that the management has in its own operating procedures. For example, the personal computer market seems to be changing day by day with new products entering the market, each one seemingly more versatile and more technologically advanced than its predecessors. Under these circumstances, member firms will need to keep a constant check on these changes and be prepared to act accordingly.

In contrast, a firm that deals with a single product line and just a small number of customers in a fairly stable market, may see little need for a complex monitoring system. For example, market changes may be signalled well in advance and a relatively low volume of business transactions may require little more than a regular, manual inspection of performance.

However, marketing planning should be viewed as a continuous operation and if it is to be implemented effectively, it should be accompanied by some regular system of measurement and control.

Travelway Ltd (E)

Travelway's conscious effort to increase market share in 1986 had the backing of an existing computerized, sales analysis system. Ronald Finlay commented:

'Being able to analyse sales quickly and over several factors gives me a feeling of having a 'finger on the pulse'. As nearly everything goes through the computer it's simple enough to code transactions by individual operator, holiday type, agency location, etc. In allocating operating expenses and overheads to the various product areas, I can get a much better picture of how well the individual units of the business are performing.

'In this way, I can act relatively quickly if an adverse trend shows up or I can measure the effectiveness of some pre-planned change in strategy. For example, I kept a careful check of the expenditure needed to push operator x's tours and, over a short time period, I was able to judge the cost- effectiveness of the campaign. Had the early results not been so encouraging, at least I'd have had the confidence to cut my losses, rather than hanging on in the hope of improvement.'

Planning for the longer term

Anticipating and acting upon predicted longer-term changes in market conditions obviously increases the perceived level of risk in decision marketing. However, ignorance of long-term changes or simply thinking in the short term may involve greater risk in leaving the firm vulnerable to unforeseen threats and missed opportunities. The philosophy of planning, even in its basic form, fosters the deliberation on those market factors and company skills and resources which need careful and constant attention if the firm is to survive.

Travelway Ltd (F)

At the end of 1986, Ronald Finlay had decided to take a much longer view of the business. 'I had this feeling,' he commented, 'that certain changes were taking place but I couldn't really quantify them.'

Marketing planning

He invested in a published market report which included a section on travel agents and, after reading it, carefully he noted the following observations:

Based on sample statistics:

- There had been a significant increase in holiday bookings by persons in the 20-24 and 25-34 age groups between 1984 and 1986.
- Overall visits to travel agents to collect brochures had decreased by nearly 25 per cent over the same period.
- There was a 50 per cent increase in booking at travel agencies by the AB class of consumer (professional, executive group).
- A greater number of females appeared to be booking holidays (increase of nearly 50 per cent over 1984).
- The business travel sector was predicted to grow.

He also noted that, for the longer term, tour operators were likely to increase their operations in dealing directly with the public and that own-label holidays sold by some of the larger agents would increase. Added to this, it was anticipated that restrictions on commission regulation could well be abolished. 'If these trends continue and the predictions materialize,' he responded, 'there is

Opportunities	Threats
• growth in business travel • growth in AB tour bookings • growth in young adult bookings • swing to self-catering holidays (flight-only opportunities)	• operators moving into high street agencies • expansion by larger agencies • large agency less than 10 miles away • abolition of discount restrictions
• comparatively small	• existing 'loyal' customer base • relative geographical (regional) coverage • flight-only operation • latest technology for enquiries, bookings and reservations
Weaknesses	Strengths

Figure 4.2 Travelway: SWOT analysis

Marketing in Small Businesses

no way I could sustain the growth in the business or perhaps even survive, unless I am prepared to change with the tide.'

As a first step he mapped out a SWOT (*S*trengths, *W*eaknesses, *O*pportunities, *T*hreats) analysis (see Figure 4.2).

He then deliberated:

'What I need to do is to take heed of the *threats* and in some way capitalize on the *opportunities*. Of course I can only achieve the latter if it corresponds with my particular *strengths*. Similarly, if I can't correct my *weaknesses* then I will need to avoid any strategy which exposes these.

'There are obviously a number of alternative routes I could take. The choice is really through a process of eliminating the lesser-attractive alternatives, until I'm left with the most attractive route(s). Of course I would like to pursue all of the opportunities, but my resources are somewhat limited.'

In the end, Ronald Finlay realized that the long-term threats of operators increasing their hold on retailing and the power of the larger agencies plus the possibility of a discounting war, could seriously affect his future business. To lose market share in this sector would significantly affect profitability, as it represented some 40 per cent of his total business. As a preliminary move, he prepared the outline plan shown in Figure 4.3.

Conclusion

Such a systematic approach to planning may not suit or be readily applicable to all small enterprises and it would be folly to assume that all things will automatically go to plan. However, the very act of planning itself will tend to focus attention on crucial environmental and internal (company) issues, in addition to providing a yardstick for performance measurement and control.

Checklist
- What are the key market trends, e.g. customers, competition?
- What are the key threats and opportunities, current and predicted?
- What are the firm's major strengths and weaknesses?
- How does the firm compare with its immediate competitors?
- What opportunities match the firm's key strengths and avoid its major weaknesses?
- In light of the above analysis, what marketing objective is realistically achievable and over what time horizon?
- Which is the best way to achieve this objective? (Strategy)

Marketing planning

```
1.  Marketing Objective:   To increase market share of total travel market by 0.003%
                           per annum over the period 1987–1990.

2.  Marketing Strategy:  (i)   New market development and increased
                               penetration of existing markets.
              Targets:   (a)   AB segment including young adults.
                         (b)   Business travel segment.
                         (c)   Flight-only segment.

2.1  Product Strategy

     Emphasis on up-market tours, particularly for young adults.
     Selective business travel facilities.
     Extend services to include accommodation advice and booking across all relevant
        market sectors.

2.2  Promotional Objectives

     (i)   To increase level of awareness of Travelway among AB groups
           (Business and Leisure).

     (ii)  To promote quality image.

     (iii) To develop and sustain 'brand loyalty'.
```

Projections	1987	1988	1989	1990
Total Market (£bn)	4.5	4.7	5.2	5.7
Market Share (%)*	0.063	0.069	0.072	0.075
Gross Sales (£m)	2.84	3.24	3.74	4.27
Commission = 9% of Gross Sales (£'000)	256	292	337	584
Marketing Budget (£'000)	13	15	17	20

* Assumes constant ratio between national and local growth

Figure 4.3 Travelway: marketing plan

- What market segment or segments are worth developing?
- What attention is needed to the existing marketing mix elements?
- Is there sufficient knowledge and information available to:
    Develop the sales forecast?
    Project the associated costs?
    Compile a meaningful marketing budget?
- Is there a system whereby the marketing plan can readily be monitored for effectiveness?

Case study: Merrydown Cider[1]

Romantic images of cider making may be admirably upheld by a trip

Marketing in Small Businesses

Photo copyright: Merrydown Wine plc.

Marketing planning

to Horam Manor, East Sussex, but Merrydown, the cider company based there, is an exception in its field. Outward appearances belie the professionalism and ambition that lie at the heart of this resilient family company. Cider is both plagued and aided by popular misconceptions. Commonly regarded as a natural, rustic drink consumed by minors, winos and yokels, it is, in fact, a £340 million industry which is dominated by three large companies, H. P. Bulmer, Coates Gaymers, and Taunton.

Volume sales of cider have virtually doubled in the past ten years and now stand at around 70 million gallons. This rapid growth has aroused the interest of successive chancellors: in 1975 cider duty was reintroduced after more than forty duty-free years, and in last year's Budget it was raised by a dramatic 47 per cent. Many of the small regional producers, unable to cope with the new burden, have either fallen by the wayside or been absorbed by the big three.

The recent popularity of cider reflects the fashion for lighter alcoholic drinks. But it has also benefited from heavyweight marketing and a concerted effort to expand into the on-trade. The draught product is now available in about half of all pubs in the UK.

Powerful trio

The companies which have benefited most from this growth are Taunton (owned by a consortium of brewers which includes Courage and Bass), Coates Gaymers (an Allied-Lyons subsidiary), and Bulmer. Together, they take over 90 per cent by volume of the UK cider market. But Merrydown is not only holding its own against the giants, it is going for growth.

Having weathered the imposition of duty, Merrydown has recently emerged from the 'others' category and is now determined to establish a substantial niche for itself in the national market. 'Our objective is quite straightforward,' says Robert Howie, Merrydown's marketing director and son of its chairman and co-founder Ian Howie, 'We aim to extend our consumer franchise and create an on-trade presence.' Merrydown claims nearly 5 per cent by volume of take-home cider sales and over 2 per cent of the total market.

The company has come a long way since Howie senior and Jack Ward produced a few hundred gallons of cider in the latter's house in 1946. It has also had its fair share of luck. The house was called Merrydown, a name that has proved a valuable company asset. Horam Manor was picked up in 1947 for £1,500, and much of the company's production equipment has similarly been shrewdly and cheaply acquired.

Merrydown's history is one of opportunism and pragmatism, with periods of both struggle and growth. By 1955 its output of Vintage

Marketing in Small Businesses

Cider Apple Wine had increased from 400 to 400,000 gallons. In the same year a wine duty embracing ciders of over 15 per cent proof was imposed. This led to a 60 per cent increase in the retail price of Merrydown's product and a 50 per cent reduction in sales. 'Every crossroads is marked by an action from the Chancellor of the Exchequer,' observes Howie.

Over the next twenty years, the company survived by diversification. It introduced a range of fourteen fruit wines, cider vinegar (under the Martlet name), mead and finally apple wine again. 'It was an extremely difficult trading period,' says Howie. 'With the imposition of cider duty in 1975 we were left with Hobson's choice – produce a lower-strength drink or face extinction.'

The company responded with Merrydown Vintage, launched on to the market at just under the magic 8.5% alcohol by volume but significantly higher than most of its rivals. Vintage Dry followed two years later. Aided by the zealous marketing of the major manufacturers – which has given a boost to the whole market – Merrydown's sales flourished and national distribution in the take-home trade became established.

Indeed, the company's growth in the past decade outshines its expansion in its first. In 1981, when the unlisted securities market was set up, Merrydown, typically, leaped at the opportunity to raise capital and widen its market. It now produces 1.5 million gallons of cider a year and has a turnover of £8.2 million.

Merrydown is now approaching another watershed. Last year the cider market lost its momentum and only modest growth is forecast this year. But Merrydown, supported by grants from the EEC and the Ministry of Agriculture, is in the middle of a three-year expansion programme. This will enable it to process over 20,000 tonnes of apples – more than twice its existing requirements.

Howie says that only in October 1987 was the marketing function truly recognized and established within Merrydown. And, he claims, the fruit of this new emphasis on marketing are now emerging. This season Merrydown has rolled out a redesign for its vintage ciders. It has also begun to distribute Calvados nationally, put two new products on test and launched its final national poster campaign.

The £150,000 poster push, which broke through Dorlands, reflects Merrydown's strengths and weaknesses. Featuring the flagship Vintage products, it carries the line 'It's a sin to call it just cider. Taste it, or you'll never forgive yourself'. The clever but thinly veiled attack on standard brands is designed to distinguish Merrydown from its competition without alienating it.

Some experts estimate that the big three spent around £17 million on advertising cider last year. Merrydown, by contrast, has allocated

Marketing planning

a budget of £1.2 million for the next three years. Nevertheless, most existing Merrydown drinkers have found the products for themselves. Furthermore, the campaign is on the mark, since, as Howie puts it, 'The products' USP is their difference.'

Merrydown Vintage and Vintage Dry are strong, slightly sparkling ciders, more natural and more expensive than most. 'Unlike the major competition, vintage has no artificial sweetener, preservatives or colouring added,' explains Merrydown's production director, Chris Carr. 'They are made from dessert and culinary apples, as opposed to cider apples, and, at 8.25 per cent alcohol by volume, are stronger than most other products on the market.'

This year Vintage celebrates its tenth anniversary. 'It has created the premium sector in the market,' says Richard Purdey, Merrydown's managing director. 'To stay on top our presentation must play a part, which is why we have redesigned and installed a new labelling machine at a cost of £60,000.'

Howie agrees: 'Each company now has its entrants in the premium sector. The most recent is Diamond White from Taunton, which came on the market last autumn. It has the same alcoholic content as the Vintage ciders, and comes in a 75 cl bottle.'

While the Merrydown directors draw parallels with premium lager, the competition, despite new product launches, appears to view the cider market differently. 'The cider market is segmented in terms of style,' declares Mike Newitt, marketing director of H. P. Bulmer. 'The split is between sweet and dry.' Mike Pollak, marketing manager of Taunton, is less dismissive of the premium sector. 'Although it is still very much a sweet and dry market, there has always been a small premium sector, mainly in the off-trade,' he explains.

Merrydown claims to hold more than 30 per cent by volume of the premium sector. In 1983 sales of Vintage and Vintage Dry almost doubled and last year, despite a flat market, the company recorded a 7 per cent volume increase in sales. But, while Merrydown has enjoyed considerable success in the off-trade, the fastest growing part of the overall market has been sales in pubs and clubs, and there sales of Merrydown scarcely register. 'The on-trade is now over 50 per cent of the cider market, and we would like to establish some kind of equilibrium,' says Howie. 'We are not directly competitive with any other cider, and that is acknowledged by the producers.'

Although Merrydown argues that its Vintage products are not drunk by regular cider drinkers and would actually be of benefit to the brewers in the on-trade, it is also exploring other avenues in a bid to extend its consumer franchise. Merrydown Traditional, a medium-strength, slightly sparkling cider, is being relaunched in PET and joined by Merrydown Country. On test for the first time this

Marketing in Small Businesses

summer, Country is the first cider from the Sussex company to use cider apples. Also on test is Apple Spark, a juice designed to appeal to adults. 'It is a conscious me-too to Appletise, Kiri and Piermont,' admits Purdey. Country is due to go national next year, and a beady eye is being kept on the fruit juice sector.

Although Merrydown appears to be making tentative steps towards the mainstream market, it is wary of the new forms of packaging and has little money for speculative ventures. It has recently delisted the three-litre bag in box, primarily because of its short shelf life. On the other hand, it has put some products into PET, which now accounts for over 50% of total grocery cider sales, and is exploring the possibilities of a ten-litre bag in box for the on-trade.

Draught keg, which is favoured by the major manufacturers, is too expensive for Merrydown to contemplate. 'Draught would not only crucify us financially,' says Purdey, 'it would also deprive us of opportunities for distribution. But there is a place for the ten-litre bag in box.' Merrydown is currently testing a beer engine with two ten-litre bags in an outer case for the on-trade.

Merrydown has a strong brand in Martlet and valuable links with the growing health food sector, assets which it has failed to exploit in recent years as it has concentrated on the booming cider market. It is first and foremost a cider producer and is determined to increase its sales in that area. But these other assets could prove useful as the opposition it faces is stern and its task severe. Indeed, as Merrydown's nearest competitor is more than five times its size, and the company's on-trade expansion depends on the co-operation of its rivals, some might consider that an understatement.

Points for deliberation

- What particular environmental factors are identified in the case and how have they impacted on Merrydown's business?
- How do Merrydown compete in the market?
- How is the cider market segmented?
- What are the customers actually buying?
- Are there any pointers in the case to suggest that Merrydown adopt a systematic approach to marketing planning?

Note

1 Olins, R. (1985) 'Merrydown's vintage years', *Marketing* 13 June, 25–8 (reproduced by kind permission of Haymarket Publications Ltd).

Further reading

McDonald, M. H. B. (1985) *Marketing Plans, How to Use Them*, London: Heinemann.

5 Products and services

Synopsis

Most products and services pass through various growth and decline phases, from initial introduction into the market to eventual replacement by improved versions or even extinction. A knowledge of the forces affecting such changes is paramount to both sustaining an adequate level of sales and to effective planning for new and/or improved product developments. Planning for new product development also requires a systematic approach which takes into account the impact on the firm's resources and the inherent uncertainties in judging the likely market response. As far as possible, all reasonable measures should be taken to reduce such uncertainty, rather than relying on subjective assessment or a limited, objective appraisal.

Concept of the product life cycle (PLC)

The notion that products pass through various pre-determined stages between birth and ultimate death is well documented. This life-cycle concept (Figure 5.1) has been suggested as a useful tool for designing and implementing product and marketing strategies but this assumes that the stage of the life cycle can readily be determined at any point in time.

As the product passes through its various stages, changing market forces will compel the firm to react in some way:
- *Introduction and market development.* Given that it takes time and resources to develop market awareness, interest and the confidence to purchase, it can be expected that initial growth will be slow and thus profitability may be negative or at best very low.
- *Growth and early maturity.* In the early growth stage and usually before significant competition has time to develop, unit profits will generally attain their peak. During late growth and toward

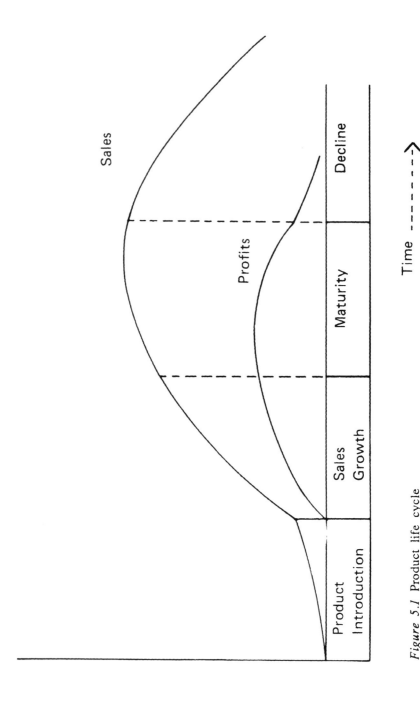

Figure 5.1 Product life cycle

Products and services

early maturity, increased competition will generally lead to reduced profit margins, probably through price cutting and other resource-hungry activities designed to ward off competition (e.g. promotion and product improvement/differentiation).
- *Maturity.* Here we can expect a saturation of competitive offerings and the limit of product improvements. Thus, sustaining market share will be the order of the day, often at the expense of profitability.
- *Decline.* As the product moves towards obsolescence and substitute products gain market share, a declining volume will tend to erode profitability and at some point the decision to withdraw from the market may have to be made.

The time scales for the life cycle vary considerably from product to product and predictions as to developments generally require the support of past experience on the patterns of similar product categories. For example, it is not difficult to understand that fashion products will generally have a very short life cycle. While in an industry based on slow technological change (e.g. building materials) life cycles will be very much longer.

What is clear is that the recognition of ultimate product obsolescence must be accompanied by a preparedness for change and this will require commitment both to continuous monitoring of sales performance and evaluation of alternative or improved products. What exactly constitutes new product development is however, arguable. A new product for the firm (e.g. diversification) is not necessarily a new product for the market at which it is aimed and a product designed to replace some existing offering by the firm may vary in its degree of innovativeness.

For example, in the washing-machine market we have seen incremental improvements in product design and technology over the past three decades or so, rather than what could be classed as major innovations. This has led to relatively long product life cycles for the various types of machines such as the early wringer, the twin-tub and the front-loading automatic.

In Figure 5.2 it will be seen that in 1964 the wringer machine still had some 20 per cent of the UK market, even after the start of the decline of the twin-tub, and the projections (1965–74) were indicating a smaller, but stable share for at least ten years into the future.

Turning to a more recent picture the continuing decline of the twin-tub and 'other' machines is evident, as is the slow-down in growth rate for automatics (Figure 5.3). Comparing Figures 5.2 and 5.3 it will also be noted that Hoover's projections to 1974 were not that far off the mark; as an approximation the market comparisons are:

Marketing in Small Businesses

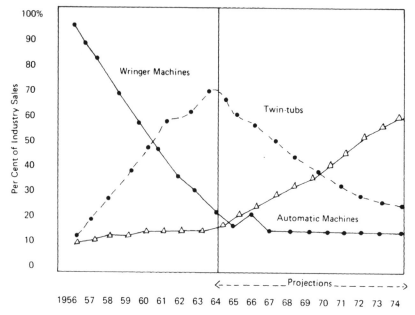

Figure 5.2 UK washing-machine market, 1956–64
Source: Hoover Limited, market research department estimates

	Projected (%)	1974 Actual (%)
Wringers (other)	10	7
Twin-tubs	32	38
Automatics	58	55

With these changing patterns some assumptions can be made regarding the impact of technology and the changes in consumer life style. On the one hand, sophisticated developments in mechanical and electronics technology have provided a means of significantly reducing the chore of washing clothes in the home and this has been helped to a large extent by consumer demand for 'convenience'.

Marketing strategy and the PLC

According to the relative innovativeness of the product on introduction to the market, it can be expected to undergo an initial resistance to purchase and ultimately, pressure from competition. Inevitably, the firm must be prepared to adjust the marketing strategy over the life cycle as these influences build up over time. Figure 5.4 gives an indication of these impacts and the changing nature of the strategy, but it is by no means the perfect answer to every situation.

82

Products and services

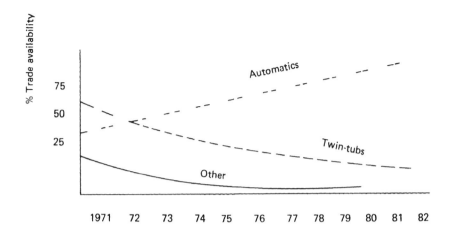

Figure 5.3 UK washing-machine market 1971–82
Source: Compiled from *Mintel* Reports and authors' estimates.

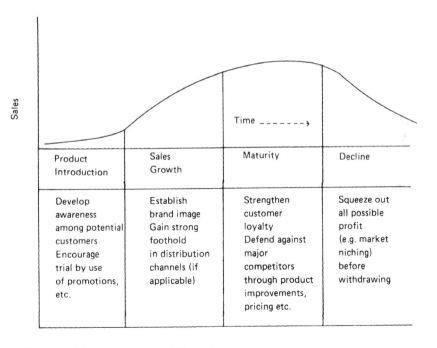

Figure 5.4 Strategy over the life cycle

83

Marketing in Small Businesses

At the introduction stage it may be necessary to single out particular customer groups, in order to target promotional effort and to set an appropriate price level. As growth builds up, further markets may be developed and as maturity approaches, attention to product variations and pricing may be needed to sustain market share. When decline occurs it may still be possible to sustain reasonable profitability by concentrating on one or two market segments (niching) for a limited period.

New product development

Product strategy

Determining product strategy is the first stage in the product development process. In basic terms this should somehow relate to the definition of the business such that new or improved products can be evaluated within the context of fulfilling customer needs and/or problem solving. This market perspective tends to broaden the horizons for product opportunity, provided it is balanced by an understanding of what the firm is capable of achieving given limited resources. For example, defining one's business as the 'manufacture and supply of quality press tools' may be more restrictive in terms of product strategy than say, 'providing solutions to the problem of complex component manufacture'. The latter gives more latitude for product development although the extent to which it can be taken will be governed by the resources and expertise at the firm's disposal.

Defining the nature of the business in this way can help to sharpen strategy and will generally restrict product development to those areas which better contribute to the overall experience effect. This relates to the ultimate cost savings which arise from the experience of dealing with the familiar over time and from providing relatively large volumes of the same products or services (economics of scale).

It is also wise to consider any new product development in the context of existing products and markets. For example, seasonality factors, supplier implications, demands on personnel (particularly salesmen), production facilities, distribution strengths and weaknesses, and any general uncertainties which the new venture is liable to generate.

Product-development process

Once the basic strategy has been agreed the process for new or improved product-development process should follow, and be contained within this framework. In very basic terms the framework

Products and services

outlined in Figure 5.5 will provide a logical set of guidelines, although it is appreciated that some deviation from this process may be inevitable, given the particular circumstances of the firm.

Formulating product ideas

At this stage no reasonable source of ideas should be ignored. The use of employees e.g. salesmen, knowledge of competitors' offerings, personal intuition, and customers' suggestions should be explored as far as possible for ideas on new or improved products. Even though this may seem a free-wheeling process it is often the start of possible innovations and in any event, the subsequent processes are designed to filter out the unfeasible. Never underestimate the views of others who apparently have little part to play in this process on the grounds that it is a restricted responsibility area. Many a large company has found it to its credit – and profitability – that shopfloor workers often have good ideas – as the suggestion box has proved time and again.

Idea evaluation and selection

The considerations of product strategy previously discussed should aid the process of filtering through those ideas which have some credibility. True, more information will be needed before any firm commitment is decided upon but at least further explanation will be narrowed down to those ideas which have a better chance of success. Likewise, this product-idea screening process will likely develop confidence as convergence of opinion approaches. This assumes, of course, that an appropriate feedback system among the original idea generators is in operation. A personal obsession with an idea to the exclusion of the opinions of others may spell trouble, as we have observed on a number of occasions. If the reader is aware that something like 80 per cent of new products fail somewhere along the line, then it might serve as a warning towards taking the more subjective approach.

Testing the product concept

As a forerunner to developing the product prototype it is useful to define and fine-tune the *concept* of what particular set of customer benefits will accrue from use of the finalized product. This is even more important where the product is to be launched on to a market which is already served by similar, competing products and thus, any new offering must be seen to be differentiated if it is to have any chance of success.

The product concept is very much to do with customers' perceptions of potential product attributes and thus is largely subjective. It is also a relative judgement, for there are probably few

Task	Action/Information Sources	Analyse
Generate new product ideas	Customers; salesmen; distributors; own staff; trade associations; licence opportunity?, competitors	Nature of the business?
Screen and select ideas	Industry reports Own staff Local library/edn establishments Internal (company) information	Existing products? Competition? Life cycle? Own resources?
Concept testing	Existing and potential customers Own staff	Customer needs? Problem solving? Product position?
Develop prototype	Internal resources Outside help	Design? Branding? Packaging?
Test prototype product and pricing etc.	Potential customers	Product? Price? Distribution? Promotion?
Modify?	Feedback from market	Marketing - mix
Launch		Market positioning

Figure 5.5 New product development programme

Products and services

cases, if any, where a set of particular needs can only be satisfied from a single source of supply. The key characteristics that a customer seeks in a particular product category may not readily be identifiable and thus the marketer must be prepared to search out and clarify these issues before embarking on the next stage of the development process. Putting a meaning to the product idea is the first stage in building what is hoped will be an acceptable identity for the longer term.

Consider the following descriptions:

1 A light, fluffy gateau made from the finest ingredients with a nutritious filling and free from artificial additives.
2 A range of compact electric motors with built-in overload protection designed for attachment to BS couplings and offered in six different sizes up to 3 hp – available from all major distributors.

Although little is conveyed – in either of these product concepts – as to the actual specifications, testing with potential customers will provide a means of evaluating the ideas and assessing whether the key characteristics have been identified. In the former case quality, nutrition, and lack of additives may be the important characteristics which will differentiate the potential product from existing competitive offerings. With the latter, it may be the perceived total 'package' rather than any other combination of individual characteristics. In the event, testing ideas at this early stage in the development process will generally provide valuable feedback, while creating an ideal opportunity to evaluate competitive offerings.

Product positioning

Understanding where the finalized product is to be positioned in the market is the key to ensuring the best possible chance of securing a competitive edge. For example, contact with potential customers and some preliminary desk research may provide sufficient information on existing product offerings, which will enable useful comparisons to be made.

Figure 5.6 shows how this type of information can be represented to provide an indication of how comparisons may be mapped out. As an example of how to interpret the maps, for the gateaux market any new product should avoid positioning too near existing brands unless it was felt that a distinct advantage could be gained using other elements of the marketing mix (e.g. pricing). Similarly, if the original electric motor concept seemed acceptable following customer research, then competitor C would deserve further attention (e.g. has he any noticeable weaknesses or strengths?). With industrial-type

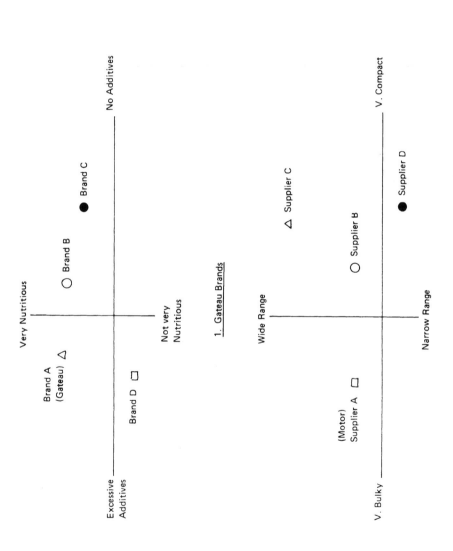

Figure 5.6 Brand and supplier positionings

products, in particular, it is often necessary to go much deeper into concept refinement, even to the point of drawing up some preliminary specifications and/or producing working models. The extent to which the firm commits more resources to research at this stage is a matter of trade-off between more expense or living with greater uncertainty. Uncertainty will be there anyway, at least until the offering is available to the market, and in following the product development sequence as fully as resources will allow, it can be assumed that everything feasible has been done to reduce the level of uncertainty.

Estimating demand and profitability

There are many sophisticated techniques available for estimating future sales, although all of them rely on either past data on sales and/or extensive knowledge of the make up of the market and customer behaviour patterns. With new products of course, we don't have the benefit of the former and our knowledge of the latter will depend on several factors such as any previous dealings with the specific market, the size, and geographical spread of the potential customer (end-user) base, the extent of competition, and the relative attraction of the proposed 'package' offering.

The need for comprehensive marketing information is stressed throughout the text and it is worth reiterating here, if only to point out the importance of providing as much support as is feasible, for the sales forecast. Too often, the rationale behind projections is based on estimations of production capacity, which assumes that the market will take whatever the firm can produce. Even if feedback from product concept testing has been very favourable it is wise to get, as far as possible, a quantitative view of the market potential. Apart from the personal satisfaction and hopefully, extra confidence gained from this exercise, any subsequent application for external funding will be better supported and argued.

Firstly, an estimate of the overall size of the market is needed and a decision on the best way to divide the market into its various segments. The size of the task will obviously depend on the nature of the product or service to be developed and the geographical spread of customers. For example, an engineering company considering developing a general engineering maintenance facility might well regard any user of machinery as a potential customer. However, there is invariably some characteristic about the business that will enable a segmentation approach to the problem, even if this is initially on a geographic basis only. The reasons for segmenting the market into distinct customer groups become more apparent when deciding on the initial marketing strategy, as we must expect some variation between each defined segment with regard to size, purchasing behaviour, needs, etc. (see Chapter 3).

Secondly, estimates of likely market penetration rates should be made, taking into account pricing policy, selling effort (including promotional expenditure), likely impact of distributors, agents etc. (if appropriate) and competitors' activity. As a further measure, repeat and/or replacement purchasing should be considered as part of the overall estimate given that the actual planning time horizon is likely to accommodate this activity.

In building up this forecast it should be borne in mind that demand is partly in the hands of the firm through the manipulation of controllable factors such as pricing and promotion. While it may be difficult to quantify the effect on sales of these elements of the marketing mix, this should never be the excuse for opting for the less-problematic method of, say, cost-plus pricing or setting a promotional budget solely based on what might be affordable at the time.

Developing the prototype

This can be a crucial stage for the small business and the level of risk is very much dependent on the nature of the product. Even if previous stages in the development process have built up the confidence to carry on, the realization that investment has now to be committed in the face of uncertainty is not always easy to come to terms with.

Whatever the size and nature of the task involved, the process of development should be guided by the characteristics defined at the product concept stage. That is, to concentrate on building up the specific attributes which come closest to identified customer needs and which will ultimately provide the necessary competitive edge. Thus, research and development should not be viewed just as a technical process, but should consciously focus on ultimate market acceptability. It is all too easy to become obsessed with the technical factors and to lose sight of the original aims, particularly where technical personnel predominate in the firm. Customers are unlikely to appreciate the effort that has gone into development as they are primarily concerned with their own needs and wants and in the main, will select those offerings that will give the best satisfaction.

As part of the development process attention should also be given to:
- *Design*. Functional and aesthetic considerations; quality aspects; legal aspects (e.g. product-liability implications).
- *Branding*. Appending a name which conveys the characteristics and benefits sought by the customer.

- *Packaging.* Attention to visual appeal; protective considerations.
- *Product launch.* The investment required at this final stage of the process will depend to a large extent on the nature of the product or service developed and some preconceived strategy on the desired rate of market penetration. Investment in tooling and materials, a new building, say, training of existing staff, possibly hiring new staff and communicating with the target audience. Whatever activities are necessary it is essential that they form part of a smooth and co-ordinated plan which is based on a previous evaluation of the market and which recognizes the likely impact on resources. The plan should spell out as far as possible, how the market is to be developed and what rate of expansion is to be achieved, over time.

Unless the product or service is truly innovative it is wise to be cautious with regard to the initial reaction of the market to the new offering. It is one thing for the firm to be convinced of the competitiveness of its product and quite another to convince potential customers. Very likely the firm will have to face problems of overcoming entrenched customer/supplier loyalties, apart from the obvious ones of lack of awareness and doubt. A planned and progressive communication programme is vital at this stage and it is important to recognize that whatever customer target group is addressed, acceptance of the product – on a sufficiently wide scale – will be a gradual process.

The communication process is covered in Chapter 8 and it suffices at this point to emphasize that trying to force adoption of the product too much, will often lead to misapplied and thus wasted resources.

Alternative sources of development

For the small business lacking particular resources and facilities, e.g. in a start-up situation, it may be necessary to consider some form of external help, whether this be in design, manufacture, marketing, or providing new products. Licensing-in tested designs will obviously eliminate the need for lengthy and expensive research and development, although responsibility for prototype development and manufacture, will still have to be assumed. Government initiatives in encouraging the high-technology industries and in particular small firms, have provided opportunities for new-starts in this area although some would argue that not enough resources have been allocated. The growth in DTI initiatives, local authority development corporations and the increasing involvement of academic establishments in the

Marketing in Small Businesses

local business community have, collectively, broadened the scope for small-business advisory services and sources of practical help.

Consideration of these alternative sources of aid should form part of the firm's overall product strategy and thus should be brought into the early stages of the evaluation process, rather than seen as a last resort. Many universities, polytechnics and colleges of higher education are able to offer cost-effective consultancy in one form or another and, through government-backed initiatives e.g. 'company teaching schemes', are able to work jointly with companies on sophisticated new-product development and manufacturing problems. Similarly, the Manpower Services Commission offers partly funded schemes for the small business contemplating growth through new product/market development, although such funding is generally related to the identification of management and staff training needs rather than product development per se.

The following case highlights the uncertainties inherent in the new product development process and the consequences that may arise from a lack of planning and pre-deliberation.

Arncliffe Tools Limited

Ralph Bowden had run a small tool-making firm for several years and had built up a steady business, turning over approximately £300,000 by 1985. Like many small businesses in the engineering sector the company had felt the effect of the downturn in manufacturing and there appeared to be little opportunity for growth in the existing business. The customer base was largely regional (a facet of the industry structure) and with prices being squeezed, a downturn in profitability was inevitable.

In the first half of 1983 Ralph Bowden was approached by an electro-mechanical engineer, Frank Sykes, with an idea for a new product range which was complementary to the tool-making business in that many existing customers were considered to be potential users. The devices would incorporate the latest microprocessor technology and would be built to individual customer specification.

Ralph Bowden was so impressed by Frank Sykes's ideas and his background and qualifications – a solid apprenticeship, some twenty years in mechanical and control engineering and a good B.Sc. – that he decided to take on the latter as technical director. Eventually a second company was formed to deal exclusively with the new venture.

By mid 1984 the new company was turning over

Products and services

approximately £90,000 per annum which represented work for about nine external customers (mainly contacts of Messrs Bowden and Sykes) and for the parent company. However, with excessive setting-up costs and the usual overheads the company was just marginally short of a break-even situation. With profit margins getting to a seriously low level on the tool-making side money had to be borrowed from the bank and certain equipment bought on hire purchase. Added to this, the uncertainties inherent in dealing with the new technology and with customized product development, had given rise to serious cash flow problems.

Earlier in the year Ralph Bowden had stated: 'I know my customers and my customers know me. If anything, the company is known for good-quality work and for personal service. How many companies can boast that their managing director knows each one of its customers personally? I am both managing director *and* salesman and this will be a key strength for the new business. I have never really had to advertise before, or mail potential customers, as I believe that things like this should be done on a personal level.'

Not long after this statement the new company, on advice from a business colleague, took on an unrelated development in the form of a portable building, but the project had to be abandoned when funds ran out later in the year. This was a bitter blow to Ralph Bowden for he felt sure that there was a lucrative market to be tapped, particularly as he considered there were no comparable products in the UK.

By early 1986 the company was looking to sustain the new venture by seeking further borrowings. The growth in the customer base was far below expectations and certain work in progress was held up. On the bright side the tool-making business was beginning to turn round but not sufficient to finance the new product venture.

Frank Sykes had been pressing for some marketing support since the setting up of the new company, but Ralph Bowden had resisted this. His (Frank's) time was largely taken up by the technical side but he readily admitted that sales and marketing were by no means his strengths.

When all attempts to get additional funding failed, Frank Sykes realized that the writing was on the wall. There was no bitterness in the parting only regret at what might have been had things gone right. Frank's final comment was: 'If only we could have built up the customer base we would now be home and dry.' Ralph remarked: 'There is really no justice for small firms like ourselves who want to branch out. Government funding in new technology is hardly worthwhile and the usual sources of finance just don't seem to care or want to understand.'

Conclusion

The company had obvious strengths with existing market contacts and Frank Sykes's experience. However, the uncertainty inherent in dealing with the new technology, the lack of an adequate order book and the customized nature of the work compounded to produce a problematic situation. Even with a larger customer base it is questionable whether the new venture could have been profitable, for this would have merely added more customized work, bringing with it more cash-eating developments. Yet, in view of Ralph Bowden's determination to stick to personal calls, it is unlikely that any attempt to create widespread awareness (i.e. at the introductory stage of product life cycle) was made. We must then question how many of his calls were actually wasted.

It was evident that the venture had not been fully thought through and consideration of a checklist prior to launch might have at least provided some forewarning. The company had a good idea – or so it seemed – but it appeared that little customer research had been implemented, which in view of the firm's closeness to the market seems surprising. Such research could have been done at the concept-testing stage and useful feedback obtained. The venture never really got much beyond the market development stage and as this by nature would have been lengthy, then initial sustained losses and cash flow problems might to some extent have been predicted (one use of the PLC!).

Where a relatively high level of investment is needed to get a new idea off the ground, it is simply not enough to rely on a purely personal conviction. Research shows that on average, some 80 per cent of new product ventures fall by the wayside at some stage of development. Wherever possible, the systematic, objective approach described previously should be applied.

Checklist

- *Impact on present products.* Will the development enhance the sales and profitability of the firm's total line (although small marginal marketing and overhead costs associated with production and sales are not always possible)?
- *Research and development.* With regard to any technical

Products and services

complexities can company resources and expertise cope or is outside help necessary?
- *Manufacture.* To what extent can the product be standardized and does the potential volume (demand) suit existing facilities?
- *Cyclic implications.* Does the current product line have seasonal demand peaks and if so, can temporarily idle resources be utilized?
- *Supplies.* Does the firm have any sort of control over supplies and can this be enhanced through the new venture? If new sources of supply are needed are there any implications for vulnerability?
- *Channels of distribution.* Would the new venture mean establishing and developing new relationships or can existing channels be used effectively?
- *Level of investment.* Given the estimated level of investment how would the firm stand among established competitors? (By assessing the industry structure it is possible to get some idea of the likely investment needed to compete effectively.)
- *Management and marketing skills.* What type of people are needed for successful new-product development and launch? Are there any technological (product/application) factors where particular selling capabilities will be required?

Can the present management cope with the potential changes and handle the type of decision making that will be needed?

Although not all the answers may be provided, this checklist will aid the evaluation of ventures that take the firm beyond the relatively familiar domain of existing markets and products.

Case study: Fire-Mann (Sales) Ltd[1]

Fire-Mann (Sales) Ltd is a progressive Manx Company fully committed to making the environment safer through the prevention of fire. The company's mainstream activity is the manufacture and marketing of an advanced range of fire-retardant chemicals. The products are the culmination of several years' research and development. In essence, a fire-retardant compound is used to render a flammable, and hence hazardous, material safe by reducing or preventing the chance of ignition.

The history of the company dates back several years with much of this time being devoted solely to product development but it is only in the last two and a half years that the developed products have been marketed worldwide. The measure of any product's worth has to be its success in the market place. The Fire-Mann retardants are showing themselves to be formidable contenders in world market terms, with a

Marketing in Small Businesses

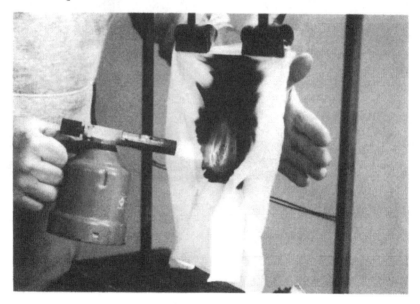

Photo Copyright: Fire-Mann (Sales) Ltd, Douglas, Isle of Man, 1988.

phenomenal growth pattern over the two-and-a-half-year marketing phase of the company's development. Success has been achieved as a result of a structured and patient progression through various stages of certification, customer presentations and hence, to the obtaining of prestigious starter contracts. All sectors of the market from the large industrial customer to the one-off in-situ treatment customer, are now being successfully serviced with the range of retardants.

The company could be forgiven for resting on its laurels, and capitalizing solely on its past research and development programme. Policy, however, is one of continued reinvestment, leading to a dynamic ongoing research programme with even more exciting products in various stages of development. The company is in a highly productive stage of its development with research being very closely linked to market demands.

From the outset, the marketing policy was to look further afield than just the British Isles. Export business is conducted through resident agent companies, and sales have been achieved in Turkey, Saudi Arabia, the United Arab Emirates, Sweden, Belgium, Holland, and West Germany. Success in these areas has led to numerous enquiries from other parts of the world. Business within the United Kingdom is conducted through an associate company, Fire Shield Services, based in Bredbury, Stockport.

Fire Shield Services

This association ensures speedy, responsive and on-the-spot representation for United Kingdom customers. Within the British Isles the retardant range is marketed under the Fire Shield trade name. A wide range of materials have already been successfully treated, with many other applications under consideration. The retardant range is consistently proving to be a market leader in terms both of performance and economic cost of treatment.

The case for fire prevention is compelling, both in terms of human safety and in minimizing commercial loss. The most obvious form of fire prevention has to be to make environments as non-combustible as possible in the first place. There is a growing awareness amongst legislators, that many everyday materials and structures are inherently combustible and unsafe. In a perfect world legislation would be in advance of tragedy, but all too often major fires and loss of life precede fire safety legislation. Higher flammability standards for structures and materials are now being introduced worldwide. The needs and demands for effective fire-retardant treatments are increasing in direct proportion to newly passed legislation.

Many people are unaware of the capabilities of fire retardants, and much remains to be done on the educational front. Flame retardants tend to be very visual products, and demonstrations are more effective than any number of spoken words. Both customer and manufacturer are immediately convinced, for example, with a demonstration on a child's cotton dress. The initial reaction is usually one of horror on seeing an example of how easily an untreated garment will ignite and burn, and one of amazement when the garment, after treatment, is subjected to a blowlamp without catching alight.

On a lighter note, the impact of visual exposure was amply demonstrated with a recent BBC *Tomorrow's World* exposé of the product. The application was a simple one with a retardant treated Kleenex Tissue used to protect £1,000 in notes from a blowlamp flame. Judging by the number of enquiries, this simple demonstration struck an immediate chord with many people.

Not all demonstrations are as dramatic as the child's dress or the Kleenex Tissue. With more difficult materials, the effect of retardant might be to reduce the chances of ignition and to slow down the rate of combustion. The value of the result should never be undervalued, as it might well mean a previously unacceptable material coming into an acceptable category. The range of materials that may be treated with retardant is highly diverse.

Fire-Mann as a company is dedicated to finding correct solutions to customers' problems. Successful applications require a close liaison between manufacturer and customer. Once customers' needs and objectives are fully highlighted, the full resources of Fire-Mann (Sales) Ltd are utilized to evaluate and produce cost-effective solutions to the problem. Enquiries are always welcome and there is normally no charge for initial laboratory evaluations.

Points for deliberation
- What would be a suitable 'business definition' for Fire-Mann?
- What factors in the case point to a 'market-orientation'?
- Who are Fire-Mann's customers and what are their needs?
- What factors have contributed to Fire-Mann's success?
- What is a key obstacle to further market development and how is this being overcome?
- To what extent have Fire-Mann adopted a formal approach to marketing planning?
- What is a key factor of Fire-Mann's product research and development?

Case study: Derwent Valley Foods[2]

In the early 1980s Roger McKechnie and his colleagues had the idea of producing exotic snacks in the belief that there was a gap in the market. All of the colleagues had experience in the savoury snack industry which was thought to be worth almost £1 billion per year. The idea had been prompted by the knowledge of the vast range of exotic snacks available in other countries from Mexico to the Far East, and the group had collected hundreds of samples from abroad to make their point.

In 1982 they contacted the venture capital group 3i and subsequently obtained additional backing to set up production on a former steel site in Consett, County Durham. Roger McKechnie and his three fellow directors Kay McGhee, Keith Gill and John Pike put up £50,000 of their own money and they raised another £400,000 which included a sum from British Steel. Later additional finance amounting to about £500,000 was provided by 3i. This gave the latter approximately a 30 per cent shareholding in the company (Derwent Valley Foods). When production started up in 1982 the first products were tortilla chips and California corn chips. The name Phileas Fogg was chosen to stress the international flavours of the brands, he being the central character in a Jules Verne novel, who went around the world in eighty days. The launch was backed by heavy advertising which focused on the Phileas Fogg connection.

The directors had wondered whether they would ever get into the

Products and services

Photo copyright: Derwent Valley Foods Ltd, 1988.

Marketing in Small Businesses

big retailers but Roger McKechnie believed that the snack industry was dominated by 'bureaucratic dinosaurs' and that the big retailers had been wanting fresh ideas and suppliers that could react quickly, for a long time. He also pointed to the focus of the snack industry on 9- to 15-year-old children and he believed that the time was ripe to attack the adult market for 'healthier' snacks.

After two years of operation the company ran into cash-flow problems as a result of over-expansion, but following a crisis meeting with Barclays Bank, one of their backers, they managed to prevent a disaster.

In 1986 the company won the CBI's business enterprise award and in 1987 the company supplied most of the leading stores, including Sainsbury, Tesco and Marks and Spencer. Profits in 1986 amounted to £500,000 on a turnover of almost £7 million with a workforce of 130. This represented nearly a doubling of sales every year and in August 1987 the company added a £1.2 million extension to the plant, allowing a doubling of the existing capacity and giving a potential through-put of fifteen million chips per day. In 1988 the company also launched a new brand, Punjab Puri, which increased the product line to ten different snacks in all.

Points for deliberation

- What are the company's strengths and weaknesses?
- How have Derwent Valley Foods segmented the market?
- What is their share of the snack market?
- What environmental factors have, or might in the future have, an effect on sales?
- How was the original product idea generated?
- What are the important 'product' features/benefits?
- What would be the approximate life cycle of the brands?
- What strategy should be adopted for Punjab Puri?

Notes

1 *Trident Magazine*, Merseyside Chamber of Commerce, September 1987, 28–9.
2 © 1987, B. Kenny.

Further reading

Lowe, J. and Crawford, N. (1984) *Technology Licensing and the Small Firm*, Aldershot: Gower Publishing.

Cowell, D. (1984) *Marketing of Services*, London: Heinemann.
Knee, D. and Walters, D. (1985) *Strategy in Retailing*, Oxford: Philip Allan.

6 Pricing

Synopsis

Pricing decisions should take account of customers' and competitors' reactions. In the former case, customers will generally perceive price as an indicator of product or service quality and will normally evaluate the cost in terms of the perceived benefits derived from the consumption of the offering. In most cases, customers have the opportunity to choose from a variety of offerings and thus price will be one of a set of comparative indicators upon which the buying decision will be based. The better the firm can differentiate its product or service from those of its immediate competitors, the more the justification for commanding a higher price, provided that this differential advantage can be sustained.

Factors affecting price

Pricing is considered to be at the heart of marketing largely because it is one side of the exchange process. Although price may seem a fundamentally rational indicator on the part of the seller, to the customer it is only one of a set of factors which are taken into account in the evaluation process. It is dependent on the nature of the product/market in question, the level and nature of competition, the perceived importance of the produce/service to the customer's needs, and, finally, the seller's overall marketing objective.

On the seller's side it is a common enough practice to price on the basis of costs plus some added percentage which represents an acceptable profit margin (cost-plus pricing). For the buyer, however, the value-for-money assessment will generally involve a host of considerations including:

- How well does the product/service meet my/our needs?

Pricing

- How well does the product/service compare with competitive offerings?
- What are the comparative cost benefits?

In addition, the potential buyer will also consider other factors such as the general ability of the seller to provide after-sales service (among others) and thus price is just one of the factors which is a consideration in the 'package offering'.

Arcady Restaurant

Adrian Stewart was in conversation with a friend in the local pub when he mentioned that a small restaurant, some five miles away from town, had been taken over by new management. The two men decided they would take their wives along for a meal that following Saturday evening, really just out of curiosity.

The restaurant was small and intimate with a plain, no-fuss atmosphere and most of the customers were in casual dress. When the waitress brought the menu, the foursome commented on the very reasonable prices, although there was some initial doubt about the impending experience to come.

With a litre of white wine, the final bill totalled less than £30, minus coffee, because the friends decided to return to Adrian Stewart's home for this last event of the evening.

Much of the conversation was centred around the night's experience and Adrian Stewart commented:

'I thoroughly enjoyed the meal and the relaxed surroundings.'

'The staff made you feel as if you were somebody and somehow the characters in there contributed to the atmosphere.'

'No problems over the price and I wouldn't have really objected to paying half as much again – which for a Yorkshireman is saying something!'

'Just think of it ... no parking problems, decent menu, good service and at last a place that doesn't over-price the wine ... when are we going again?'

Conclusion

It is clear that Adrian Stewart judged the price in terms of the 'total package' offering. We might conclude from this example that the restaurant would have some latitude for reconsidering the

Marketing in Small Businesses

price structure in view of the high degree of customer satisfaction achieved.

However, it is pertinent to note that Adrian Stewart was evaluating the event on a comparative basis and was therefore, bringing to bear previous experiences and knowledge of competitive offerings. Although he had stated that he would have been prepared to pay as half as much again, the implications for repricing might have dire consequences for the Arcady Restaurant. The lesson to be learned is in the initial pricing, and this should take into account customers needs, expectations and the effect of competition.

New product pricing

If the product offering is considered unique, then even more deliberation is needed, as the following case illustrates:

A novel securing device

David Jackson was a sole trader, manufacturing and supplying waterproof clothing for use by outdoor workers and sportsmen, etc. Having supplied a number of local window-cleaners with his products he had noted over the years, the practice of securing and conveying ladders on the roofs of vehicles. Believing that there was a need for a more convenient method of securing and releasing ladders he developed, with the help of a friend, a clamping device which could readily be fitted to vehicle roof-racks.

From observation, David Jackson concluded that the present methods, ranging from securing with ropes or leather straps to use of screw clamps, were unnecessarily time-consuming and particularly cumbersome in wet weather conditions. He stated:

'My device is very simple to use. The ladder can be clamped in a matter of seconds and can be released in much the same time. There is a facility for fitting a padlock and so it is much more secure than any present method. The clamp could be fitted to walls and thus ladders could be made secure when not in use. I imagine that anyone who has a need to convey ladders will find the device very useful. Painters and decorators, window-cleaners, British Telecom engineers and house builders and repairers.'

He had contacted a number of small, regional distributors who had indicated a willingness to stock samples for a trial period. In

Pricing

deciding on pricing David Jackson worked on a cost-plus basis. He felt that he had got the best deal from his local sub-contractors (wisely, he had arranged for the various individual components to be produced by different companies so that no company would have access to the complete design). With the estimated distributors' margin and his own profit, he concluded that the maximum retail price should be around £10. His main argument was that users would question any higher price on the basis of the simplicity of design and the small amount of materials which made up the clamp.

The one major competitive product he had identified worked on the basis of a screw-down type clamp which was judged to be rather time-consuming and this was priced at around £11.

Conclusion

Although David Jackson had thought about some of the market implications for pricing, e.g. distributor margin and user perception, he was basically concerned with a cost-plus approach. Ignoring the factors of user benefits and competitive advantage may often lead to under-pricing. In the end, the user will tend to compare the cost of purchase with the benefits from use of the product and with alternative offerings. The assumption that users would somehow have the ability to estimate the material and production costs is very questionable and is a clear sign of a lack of a 'customer-need' orientation.

Although it turned out that David Jackson had tested out the idea with a number of potential users, he had not used this opportunity to assess just what price (maximum) they would be prepared to pay. Likewise, he appeared to have ignored the time and money spent in developing and promoting the product and thus, the justification for initially pricing to recoup these costs.

In deliberately pricing below the screw-clamp device he believed that potential customers, already aware of the latter product, would see this as an added attraction. However, there are times when quality and performance are, in the customer's mind, linked with price and thus an unexpectedly low price may indicate inferiority in some way.

Pricing policy

With established businesses problems may occur due to changing market conditions and the symptoms may build up to a dangerous level, before the company has recognized the chief causes:

Marketing in Small Businesses

Chem-Tech Laboratory Supplies

In 1985 Richard Maddison was facing a financial crisis. From a steady profit position some three years earlier the company had run up a considerable bank overdraft. Although he had sensed the deterioration in the business he readily admitted that he couldn't put his finger on the cause and that some drastic action was needed.

Part of the problem had been that Richard Maddison had other business interests which tended to command more of his time. Thus the laboratory supplies business had virtually been in the hands of the small number of staff on-site. The latter comprised the buyer, field salesman, store-keeper, two staff involved in packing and distribution, invoice clerk, and a van driver. In addition, three part-time staff were involved in various office duties. It seemed that no one person was in overall charge but it was acknowledged that Bob Chilton, the buyer, having been with the company since its formation, was generally looked to as the office manager. He was responsible for pricing and had set a pricing policy which had not really changed over the years. This involved a standard mark-up on the cost-price with no charge for packing and postage. Bob Chilton commented: 'I have been with the company many years and I've built up a good relationship with suppliers. This gives us in the end, a very high customer service level and we have a good reputation for responding quickly.'

Alan Fieldhouse, the salesman, had been with the company for less than two years. Although somewhat on the young side, he was keen and ambitious. However, he had been in conflict with Bob Chilton over the loss of one or two major accounts: 'We lost the business because we couldn't offer competitive discounts,' commented Alan Fieldhouse. 'I had managed to sustain a number of accounts by offering attractive discounts but then I was overruled. If I was given the responsibility, I could really start to build the business up.'

Further investigations concluded that:

- There had been a considerable swing in the balance between major and minor customer accounts over the past three years and that a larger proportion of orders were for small items distributed across the country.
- Response to customers' telephoned orders was geared to reducing lead time to an absolute minimum. In some cases the company would arrange with the wholesaler for supplies to be sent direct to the customer.

Pricing

- Average settlement period for creditors was 30 days while that from debtors was nearer 60 days.
- Average margins had been reducing over the past two years.
- Changes in the industry had resulted in the emergence of a small number of relatively powerful suppliers who were exerting price squeezes on the smaller distributors.

Conclusion

The lack of overall effective management in the company was clearly a factor in its demise. In the absence of an established pricing policy, individuals will often develop their own standards and both Alan Fieldhouse and Bob Chilton might have been forgiven for thinking they were doing the right thing.

The shift in balance towards the smaller order sizes, the attention to high customer-service level and the absence of distribution charges would, collectively, impose penalties on profitability. In view of the debtor/creditor situation it might be argued that the company would be viewed favourably by both its customers and suppliers. There would, however, seem to be some latitude for renegotiations in this respect.

The lack of management and planning appeared to be the real underlying cause of the problem, and this was reflected down to the level of pricing policy (among other things!).

This is a clear case of failing to note and act upon changes in the environment (customers and industry) and the corresponding impact on the internal organization and operations.

Competitor- and customer-oriented pricing

Of course, sometimes price can be overestimated on the basis of how the firm regards its own product or service. It is not uncommon to assume that what one is offering to customers is that much better than that offered by competitors and therefore, the price must be attractive. This is not to deny the firm's faith in its own products or to question genuine enthusiasm – which are admirable qualities – but to point to the dangers of an over-obsession with the product:

Ingson Autobodies

Rob Deverson and Keith Ingle had worked for several years for a medium-sized coachmaking firm. When the two were made redundant as a result of closure, they decided to set up on their own, customizing commercial vehicle bodies.

They had the advantage of existing customer contacts and were confident the work would be there for the taking, given their skills and the opportunities to raise the necessary capital. The partners worked hard during the first year of operation and had completed a number of jobs for customers who were on the books of their original employer. As these orders were drying up the company sought to gain new customers but this was met with little success.

Rob Deverson commented: 'I just can't understand why we can't get the extra business. We provide a high-quality, efficient service and I'm sure that no one can match us for price.'

Keith Ingle added: 'We really don't have any competition in the area – I mean, no one has our quality, delivery capability or price. In fact, we've never really considered what the other body shops might be offering – we just know from experience that we're very good at what we do and that the price we're asking is competitive. In fact, it is less than what our previous employers were charging.'

Conclusion

It should be noted that the partners were genuinely confident about the business and that neither was arrogant. However, their 'experience' base which was at the root of their convictions might be considered limited. They had the initial advantage of securing a few 'loyal' customers plus the experience gained with their former employer. The latter would give them only a narrow view of service and pricing comparisons and, of course, the actual closure of their former employer's business might be one good reason for casting doubt on any such comparisons.

In the end, it is the customer's perception of price/quality comparisons which will largely determine with whom the business is placed. Perhaps ignorance of competitors' activities could be excused, but the assumption that competition didn't really exist because of the partners' over-estimation of their own uniqueness, would place the company in a very tenuous position. As it turned out, there were at least four other similar types of operation in the area and because the service was somewhat difficult to differentiate, pricing would have been a crucial element in competing for business.

Pricing and product differentiation

Where there is some latitude for differentiating the product or service

Pricing

on offer, pricing is best set in context of the supplier's total 'package' offering, as viewed by the prospective customer. For example, the ability to deliver on time, the perceived quality of after-sales service, the supplier's credibility as a going concern and, of course, price.

Buyer – press tool company. 'We have five potential suppliers on our books ... sometimes our own customers unexpectedly change specification and so we expect a supplier of the materials concerned to respond quickly to these changes.

'In fact, only one of our suppliers seems able to respond quickly enough and, of course, we expect to pay a little more for this service.

'For the more predictable side of our business, and as a general rule, price is the main consideration so it's a question of negotiating with the remaining four suppliers.'

Housewife. 'We had a price in mind before we started to look round the fitted kitchen suppliers.

In the end, we paid a little more than anticipated because we had to be sure that the kitchen looked right.

You hear so many stories about poor workmanship and long delays, you could be throwing money away just going on price.'

Materials buyer – curtain manufacturer: 'Certain of our materials are imported from Italy.

'Even if you could get the quality here in the UK it's unlikely the manufacturers could deliver on time.

'It makes me laugh sometimes when I hear people quibble about cut-price imports ... price isn't the be-all and end-all.'

In these three examples, the buyers concerned clearly put a great deal of emphasis on the cost/benefit implications of the choices open to them. In all cases, the products were an important and essential part of the business operation or the home (in the case of the housewife). Had the toolmaking company been considering ringbinders or the housewife, drawing pins, the buying decisions would have required less deliberation. In fact, both might well have popped down to their local W.H. Smith's and thought no more of it!

Pricing at the going-rate

When it is difficult to differentiate the firm's product or service 'package' from those offered by competitors, then it may be a question of sticking to the going-rate; that is, the average industry price related to the product/market in question. Motor vehicle servicing, timber supplies, general hardware supplies, TV retailing, and heating and plumbing are all, with possibly a few exceptions, examples where average prices are largely maintained through local and/or national competition.

In such businesses it may be difficult for the individual firm to justify a higher than average price and so it becomes a question of keeping costs down as far as possible, while attempting to maintain an adequate level of service. For any firm this is a fine balancing act, particularly if there is a need to resort to price cutting in order to attract volume sales.

Amplivision

Amplivision's premises were located on the edge of town (population: 110,000) and the company were agents for several well-known manufacturers of tv, hi-fi and radio equipment.

Steve Barbour, Amplivision's managing director explained his situation:

'We're at a slight disadvantage with our location and I feel obliged to regularly advertise in order to pull the custom in. We can beat any supplier in the area on price, we stock a very wide range of modern products and carry a first-class team of qualified service engineers.

Business isn't too bad at the moment, but I feel some new approach will be necessary if we are to grow in the next two years. With the cost of stock holding and advertising, plus the need to build up the service side a little more, I'm not sure that I could cope with further price cutting.

I do realize, however, that competition doesn't stand still and that I should be taking action *now*, rather than waiting till the inevitable happens.'

Conclusion

In some ways, Amplivision's location had forced the company into differentiating its prices and regrettably, it found itself locked into a situation that it would find difficult to change. With an existing reputation for a wide product range and competitive prices and with a need to advertise, any moves to improve profit margins by adjusting one or more of these elements of the marketing mix, might well have the ultimate opposite effect. However, if competition did eventually respond by price cutting, almost certainly Amplivision would feel obliged to follow suit in order to sustain one of its key selling points.

Pricing

Checklist

- How important is the product/service to the end-user? e.g.:
   is it an essential and important entity in a business operation?
   or does it carry 'status' as far as the consumer is concerned?
- How does the end-user view price among other factors such as delivery, product quality and reliability, after-sales service, etc.?
- What is the nature and extent of competition and how does this influence price?
- Is there a 'going-rate' price level?
- Is the product/service sufficiently differentiated from competitive offerings to warrant a higher price?
- How sensitive is the market to price?
- What is the approximate market potential and what sales volumes can reasonably be expected from, say, setting prices A, B, or C?
- Given sales volumes A, B, and C (corresponding to the above prices) and evaluating the respective costs which price will realize the maximum profit?
- What are the dangers of pricing too low or pricing too high?
- If applicable, what margin would the middleman expect?

Case study: Linn Products[1]

If you are the proud owner of a new compact-disc player you will not be pleased to hear that the purists in the world of hi-fi still believe that the traditional black vinyl record produces a better and more agreeable sound than the compact disc.

And if you think that this defiance of what has almost become the conventional wisdom is just the view of a few cranks, you should know that a company named Linn Products will this year be making four times as many of its high-quality record turntables as last year. Its total sales of turntables, amplifiers and loudspeakers are rising by about 30 per cent on an annual basis, and the company expects them to reach £25 million in about five years time from last year's level of £5.5 million.

Linn Products believes it is taking off after a decade and a half of leading what amounts to a quiet revolution in the world of hi-fi equipment. Its success, soon to be confirmed by a move to a new purpose-built, automated factory, is based on a radical new approach to design, minute attention to quality and detail, and unusual attitudes to production and marketing.

Linn – it takes its name from the southern suburb of Glasgow in which it is based – is the creation of Ivor Tiefenbrun, the son of a Glaswegian mother and an Austrian father who emigrated to Scotland

111

Photo copyright: Linn Products, Eaglesham, Glasgow, 1988.

in 1939. At the beginning of the 1970s, frustrated at what he considered the poor quality of sound emerging from even the most expensive loudspeaker system, Tiefenbrun decided that the root of the problem was the poor quality of the signal coming off the record.

'There was a perception in the industry that the loudspeaker made the sound better – that even a bad signal could be improved by a good set of speakers,' he says. 'By the late 1970s I had proved to the industry that the most important thing in sound reproduction is the software – the input signal itself – and that unless you feed a good signal into the speakers you will not get good sound out of them.'

To prove his point he developed a new turntable, the Linn Sondek LP 12. It incorporates a patented bearing to support the disc and employs very high standards of precision engineering, both in the turntable and tone arm. The result is the elimination of extraneous vibration which allows the stylus to concentrate on recovering minute pieces of information from the record groove. First-time listeners found they heard music from their records that they did not know existed. Even the scratches on battered old records were less discernible.

Linn then turned its attention to loudspeakers, deciding that, as with turntables, the cause of imperfect reproduction lay in inadequate engineering which set up vibration larger than the signals they were trying to reproduce. Its first speakers, introduced in 1974, drastically cut bass resonance.

It was only after 1980 that the company began designing the predominantly electronic pre-amplifiers and power amplifiers. The aim was, in Mr Tiefenbrun's words, to 'nurture the signal which is still very delicate at this stage'. Linn's amplifiers were launched in 1985 and were the first to be controlled by microprocessors.

Linn's hi-fi equipment is not intended for the consumer who is content to buy his sound system at a multiple discount store where, says Mr Tiefenbrun:

> 'People choose equipment on its appearance or price. We only expand our retail base to keep in line with production, which is limited by the size of our plant. We prefer to be able to meet demand very speedily and maintain service, rather than to have a backlog of orders.'

In Britain, Linn sells through a network of only about ninety hi-fi dealers which meet the company's exacting standards for installing and demonstrating hi-fi equipment – Linn insists that its speakers are demonstrated in rooms without any other speakers, because it believes that the presence of other speakers distorts the sound. Exports account for nearly half the company's turnover, with the US its biggest single

Marketing in Small Businesses

export market and Japan among the top five importers of Linn equipment.

The company's products are not cheap: a complete set of the cheaper range of Linn equipment could cost about £1,500 and it is possible to spend more than £4,000. But for that price, according to Mr Roy McCullough of Russ Andrews, Linn's only dealer in Edinburgh, the customer is getting quality at least as good as that of a £20,000 US or Japanese luxury hi-fi system.

Linn may shun the mass hi-fi market, but it does not try to blind its customers with science. Unlike many other hi-fi manufacturers it does not publicize the technical specifications of its products. 'You can't tell what it's going to sound like from reading the specifications,' says Mr Tiefenbrun. 'People should decide to buy simply on the basis of whether it sounds better,' he says.

Linn believes that a revival of specialist hi-fi is under way in Britain and elsewhere, and that with its strong product range and increasingly well-known name it is well placed to take advantage of an upsurge in interest. Linn also expects a major increase in sales by stepping up its presence in foreign markets, especially in the US (where it hopes to treble sales over the next few years), West Germany, and France.

Mr Tiefenbrun says that the world market for specialist hi-fi is worth about £100 to 120 million a year, of which British companies have about half. The market is expanding by about 14 per cent a year but Linn's sales are growing at about twice that rate, outselling its UK and foreign rivals. Mr Tiefenbrun observes:

> 'People are watching less television, the video and home computing booms are over, the joggers are ageing ... more and more people want to sit back and listen to good-quality sound. Some of this new interest has been created by the boom in compact discs, which has taken a small part of the UK market and has posed a dilemma for people who have large record collections.'

Mr Tiefenbrun believes that the long playing record will be in production for at least another 10 years, and with many millions of record titles in existence the compact disc (CD) will never replace it. In the meantime, he believes, record owners are upgrading their turntables and tone arms to match or exceed CD performance. The CD, he says, is 'just another format', no more likely to destroy the record than were cassettes.

'There is more information on a record than there is on a compact disc,' he says. Many discs, he says, sound somewhat lifeless and lacking in musicality compared with a well-made record. The same is

Pricing

likely to apply to digital audio tape (DAT), the latest Japanese invention that is shortly to come to Europe. In fact, an almost messianic enthusiasm was detectable in the rabbit warren of factories and backrooms which grew haphazardly into Linn's original headquarters. The 1988 workforce of over 130 – compared with 80 a year before – included 40 mechanical and electronic engineers.

Linn works to standards of precision normally employed by toolmakers rather than consumer-goods manufacturers. It uses high-quality machinery, much of it computer controlled, and enforces ruthless quality-control standards, which recently led to the scrapping of 80 per cent of examples of a turntable component because of blemishes. Many of its employees are tradesmen and others receive in-house training.

The plant has almost as much computer power as a small university. It uses this in research, design, testing finished products, and stock control. In 1985 about 7 per cent of turnover was spent on research and development. Pretax profit in 1985 dipped to £254,000 on sales of £4.5 million, from £779,000 on sales of £4 million the year before, and was almost all reinvested.

Linn's expansion has been seriously held up by lack of adequate factory space caused by delays of several years in obtaining planning permission for a new plant at Eaglesham in the countryside south of Glasgow – delays which infuriate Mr Tiefenbrun when he sees prominent foreign companies given sites and planning permission to set up in Scotland in a matter of weeks.

It is a sign of the company's confidence that it has invested some £4.5 million in the first purpose-built plant of its kind: automated guided vehicles transport components to the stands where each worker assembles and packs an entire product, rather than using the traditional division of labour. It is an unusual system of production but the company finds it very suitable for a highly motivated workforce with a wide range of skills. As the company's newsletter to its customers states: 'The people who work in Linn are mostly hi-fi nuts or enthusiasts.'

Points for deliberation

- How has Linn Products segmented the market?
- How does the company compete in the market?
- What are the key company strengths?
- What was the basic idea behind the product development?
- What type of customer needs are being met?
- What pricing strategy has the company adopted?

Marketing in Small Businesses

Note

1 *Financial Times*, 11 March 1987 (reproduced by kind permission of Financial Times Ltd).

Further reading

Gabor, A. (1977) *Pricing, Principles, and Practice*, London: Heinemann.

7 Distribution

Synopsis

Distribution decisions involve the evaluation and selection of market intermediaries such as agents, wholesalers, and retailers. Although many small firms elect to sell directly to the end-user, in seeking growth opportunity the sheer cost of reaching a wider market may necessitate operating through one or more of these 'channels' of distribution. In doing so, the firm is not only faced with the problem of motivating channel members to accept its products, but also with increased vulnerability, as it becomes more remote from the end-user market. Essentially, distribution decisions involve a trade-off between distribution costs and marketing control.

Problem areas

For many small businesses, particularly in manufacturing, the use of middlemen such as agents, wholesalers, retailers, etc., is virtually obligatory. This poses certain pressures in terms of pricing and promotion (to the end-user) and often means long-term commitments which may or may not succeed.

Although the company may opt for the most economical method of distribution this will probably lead to much less control over its own destiny and will distance the company from the 'user market'. In the worst case the company may find itself locked into a single distributor and unless there is some mutually agreed long-term protection, either side will be vulnerable.

CroxMills Pre-packed Meats

Robert Croxall and Gary Mills had served some considerable time in the butchery trade and between them had thirty years' experience. They decided to set up in business in 1982, processing and supplying pre-packed, cooked meats. This was in the belief that they could improve on the quality and prices of the then existing suppliers and that they had good personal contacts with potential meat suppliers. Although they had secured contacts with a small number of retail outlets they soon discovered they lacked the resources and time to develop the full market potential. Business only slowly developed and by the middle of 1983 the partners realized that something drastic needed to be done if the company was to survive.

Quite out of the blue, they were contacted by a locally based wholesaling operator and, following negotiations, it transpired that the latter would be prepared to take most, if not all, of their existing output. The two sides eventually arranged a mutually agreed pricing structure and delivery schedule, although no written contractual agreement was entered into. The partners were delighted with the arrangements as not only did it secure continued employment for the twelve or so staff, but also their convictions seemed to have been fulfilled.

Regrettably, the arrangement required that the company should not supply local retailers and it was left to Gary Mills to inform the latter. Coincidentally, in the year following the agreement, the partners were contacted by a number of retailers but had to decline entering into business transactions.

Robert Croxall commented:

> 'It's a pity the products aren't connected with the CroxMills name and even the retailers, let alone the consumers, are none the wiser. We have some interesting new product ideas such as frozen pre-prepared meat dishes, but the wholesaler doesn't seem too keen. We know they carry competitive products in this line so I suppose they feel some commitment. Still, we should be thankful for small mercies.'

Towards the end of 1985 business began to fall off and, in spite of continued assurances from the wholesaling operation, orders were gradually run down to an unacceptable level. When the partners eventually confronted the wholesalers, they discovered that an alternative supplier was offering more competitive prices and that if the company wished to continue doing business they would have to review the pricing arrangements; and not only that, but no guarantees could be given regarding minimum orders. The buyer explained:

> 'We have our own situation to consider. Prices are being squeezed to an absolute minimum and local retailers are spoilt

Distribution

for choice. We try to keep to agreements but the realities of business have no room for sentiment. I'm sorry, but that's the way it is. Look at the local supermarkets and the national brands they stock ... just compare the prices and you'll realize the squeeze on our own margins.'

Some time later Gary Mills commented:

'We have a first-class product range and we can't even tell the consumer this, let alone link our name with the product. I'm not knocking our competitors but I can't believe that price is the only factor affecting choice.'

Conclusion

The moral of the case may seem obvious as it points to the dangers of putting all your eggs in one basket. However, in times of desperation the offer of a substantial amount of business may be too attractive to refuse and the possible long-term consequences may be the last thing on the company's mind.

Yet the arrangement was very much one-sided and CroxMills had not really demonstrated any bargaining power. If the distributor had considered the products worth taking on in the first place, we might assume that CroxMills would have had some latitude for negotiating and formally agreeing terms of supply. After all, they were virtually cut off from the retailer (and consumer) and were obviously willing to develop and cement loyalty with the distributor, therefore they would deserve some sort of formal commitment from the wholesaler in return for this.

Similarly, particular problems can arise when the small company acts as distributor:

Arncliffe Materials Handling

The company had been in business for five years, manufacturing and supplying specialist conveying systems. More recently, the company had added complex electronic control units to the systems and these units were imported from a Swiss-based company.

Following a business trip to Switzerland, Gordon Collie, a qualified mechanical engineer and production director, commented: 'Our supplier has offered us sole northern UK agency/distributorship for the control units. The agreement

119

Marketing in Small Businesses

requires us to carry a certain amount of stock and to move at least five units per month for the first year.'

Alan Hoggard, the managing director, also a qualified mechanical engineer, appeared delighted by the opportunity: 'I think we should jump at it. I don't think we'll have any trouble at all shifting the minimum volumes.' Gordon Collie was less optimistic but he agreed that the venture was only low-risk.

The company's main business comprised large, one-off systems, which required assembly and testing on-site. The Swiss company had advised on the interface of the electronic control units and, for the first electronically controlled system sold, had sent over an engineer to help in the installation. The nature of the work meant that two to three systems could be installed per year at best and each system would require one electronic control unit.

After the company had formally entered into agreement, Alan Hoggard commented: 'I think we were fortunate to have dealings with the Swiss company – a piece of luck visiting that Mechanical Handlings exhibition in Hanover last year. We've got a good, competitive product of our own now.'

Some six months later, the directors were beginning to feel the pinch. The only unit they had sold was for one of their own conveyor systems. They had up-dated their usual advertisement in the appropriate trade journal but were at a loss as to how to get at the wider, potential market. On top of that, exchange rate fluctuations resulted in higher-priced imports.

While visiting an installation, Gordon Collie had tried a couple of 'cold calls' in the area, but admitted they were somewhat of a disaster: 'I was directed to electronic designers in each case and I felt very uncomfortable – like a fish out of water. I couldn't give them the intimate details and besides, I only had the basic product literature which we haven't yet had translated into English.'

Conclusion

The Swiss manufacturers had obviously over-estimated Arncliffe's ability to act as competent agents. The company was ill-equipped to deal with the marketing side, as the new business bore little relationship to the existing business, other than a narrow field of application. However, it is surprising that the directors did not seek more support from the Swiss company (e.g. product literature appropriately translated), and more surprising that no attempt was made to recruit staff with the appropriate marketing/technological experience.

The assumption that the new business could simply be lumped on to the existing operation suggested that the diversification was ill-thought through.

Deciding on distribution channels

There is often conflict in deciding what channels are ideal and what is available, let alone deciding on actually how to get into suitable distributors. The obvious starting point is the market or markets the company is trying to reach and, in some cases, channels are readily identifiable, such as wholesalers and retailers in fast-moving consumer goods. However, where the market for a product may have many facets, appropriate channels may be difficult to identify and probably even more difficult to evaluate.

Economy Energy Systems

The company had developed a simple-to-install energy-measuring system which recorded the use of electrical power, and which would identify at what precise time of the day and where in the premises more-than-average consumption was occurring.

Nick Hartle, the managing director, reviewed the situation:

> 'I've sold a few systems locally and have had favourable feedback. In some cases, the users have managed to reduce quarterly electricity costs by identifying unnecessary use of power and by making departments more conscious of the need to conserve energy. The trouble is, I want to expand the new business but I don't know where to start. I suppose almost any type of business might find the system useful. I've managed to contact a couple of agents down south but, as yet, I can't see much happening.'

Conclusion

Viewing the market *en masse* has its own particular problems. Unless clearly defined segments can be identified and evaluated, it is bound to be a problem choosing appropriate channels of distribution and, indeed, deciding on other elements of the marketing mix such as pricing and promotion.

Some attempt to segment the market was necessary in this case, otherwise general marketing activity would be ill-focused and confusing. For example, what sectors of commerce and industry would be more likely to view energy conservation as a priority?

Marketing in Small Businesses

Would company size and turnover be a factor in the propensity to purchase? What sectors are growing and what sectors are declining? For the potentially attractive sectors, what are their purchasing habits and to what extent are middlemen involved?

Such an approach would provide much more confidence in dealing with the market and enable the marketing mix to be more finely tuned. The alternative, aggregate approach is generally more risky and presents an onerous task in terms of marketing monitoring and control.

Evaluating channels of distribution

Assuming the company has a choice of alternatives, the key considerations are:

- The volume of sales desired?
- The comparative costs of achieving this desired level through direct selling or through middlemen?
- How much marketing control the company can afford to lose?

In the final analysis, the best choice is generally the one that will produce maximum profits, although care should be taken regarding the possible long-term consequences, as CroxMills came to realize.

It will be appreciated that unless the product is unique, selective distribution arrangements will be virtually impossible. Thus, it is likely that whatever the choice of channel, the firm must live with the fact that distributors will probably be handling competing products. This will, no doubt, give the distributor an upperhand in negotiating terms and conditions and, in many cases, it is more than just getting the product into the distribution channel.

Track Sportswear

Track manufactured a range of tracksuits and sports bags under several suppliers' brand names. They had hit on the idea of 'sponsored' equipment which involved the printing of local company names on their products in relation to promotional campaigns, charitable events, etc.; and this proved moderately successful. However, John Dean, the managing director, had decided they should market under their own brand name. He commented: 'We have a first-class product range and can match delivery requirements with any of the big names. I don't see any reason why we shouldn't be successful.'

Following visits to a number of retailers he had somewhat modified his views:

'It's not as easy as I thought. In one shop, the manager took me round and said 'Give me one good reason why I should make shelf-space for your products? What have you got that the big names don't have?' In all honesty, I didn't have an answer other than negotiating more attractive prices. When the shop manager asked me if I could compete with Adidas's or Mitre's advertising, I just couldn't respond.'

Conclusion

John Dean had realized that to compete effectively, he had to have the appropriate brand image. Of course, there were other possible outlets for his product range, but it was unlikely that brand name, associated quality requirements, and consumer advertising would outweigh the emphasis on low price and volume through-put in these channels.

Of all the elements of the marketing mix, distribution decisions are probably the easiest to identify and to evaluate. This is largely due to the fact that many enterprises, and in particular the smaller companies, have little choice but to distribute products through the existing infrastructure. However, putting such decisions into practice is by no means an easy task and unless the product is truly innovative, the firm must be prepared to meet the competitive pressures and hard bargaining associated with the intermediary market sector.

Checklist
- Can the markets be clearly identified?
- In what way do the relevant customer segments buy?
- What alternative distribution methods are feasible?
- What are the appropriate cost implications for each alternative?
- What commitments are necessary for each of the alternatives?
- What possible long-term consequences might be involved?
- What level of marketing support is required for each alternative distribution system?
- How much marketing control will the company maintain?

Case study: Strida Ltd

Mark Sanders, a 28-year-old engineer, left the Mars Company, where he designed vending machines, and returned to college to study for a post-graduate degree in industrial design. The Strida bicycle arose from a design project idea – a folding, lightweight machine that combined appeal, functionality, and lightness. Although there were

Marketing in Small Businesses

Photo copyright: Strida Ltd, Cirencester.

similar products on the market at the time, these were considered to be cumbersome and/or difficult to unfold.

With backing from entrepreneur Paul Marshall, who in the past had managed Australian golfer Greg Norman and had spent some time forming new companies, the first production models were produced in the middle of 1987. Paul Marshall did not consider the Strida bicycle to be in direct competition with other folding models on the market. He commented:

> 'We want to market in a different way from conventional bicycles. The Strida is a very design-orientated high-tech looking machine and it's virtually maintenance-free. There's no grease anywhere on it, which means you could touch any part of the bike and come away clean.'

This marketing strategy implied that the only cycle shops that were likely to sell the Strida would be the ones who sent up their own vans to pick up stock from the warehouse. The big sales would be pitched at department and chain stores which until now hadn't considered stocking bikes and the company were looking for sales of around 8,500 in the first year and already had taken an order for 2,500 in Australia.

Two-wheeled tender[1]

Once down at the marina with your four-wheeled transport gratefully left in the car park, further movement is either conducted by boat or on foot. A meander along the quayside is normally amusing, sociable and sometimes even informative but for the quick nip round to the marina office or showers it might well be handy to be wheel-borne again. There are a number of so-called lightweight collapsible bikes around but seldom are they that light, and a degree of engineering is often required to render them safe so you don't end up on a circus unicycle.

The Strida folding 'designer' bicycle has been available since mid-summer so we thought it was time we had a closer look at one with regard to the boating and marine environment. Mark Sanders, the bike's designer, set himself some stiff design parameters, these basically being: that it should fold as opposed to collapse, into a manageable walking stick shape, without becoming a hedgehog of handlebars, pedals and assorted tubes to knock shins and catch fingers. Also that the action of folding the bike be carried out in only one or at the most two actions, and that when folded it could still be easily wheeled.

There are a number of collapsible bikes that meet some of

Marketing in Small Businesses

these requirements but few can do it with the simple style and ease of the Strida. The lower part of the frame with the pedal pulley unclips from the forward bar and rests on the ground, the front tube then swings back and the hubs locate to form a single wheel. The pulley bar can then be brought up to clip alongside the other parts of the frame.

The drive from the pedals is transferred to the back wheel by a toothed rubber belt, not the conventional chain and sprocket, and with all bearings fully encapsulated there's no grease or oil to cover blazer and flannels on the way to the yacht club. The padded seat adjusts for height with an Allen key which is neatly and securely locked under the seat itself. A parcel rack situated on the rear of the bike below the seat will hold a small bag of groceries, to save those tired arms lugging the inevitable forgotten victuals back to the boat. With a bit of boater's DIY the rack could probably be made more versatile to carry larger loads.

The Strida has no gears, unlike some of its rivals, but on the whole the pedal-to-drive ratio enables the rider to master any reasonable gradient of hill but still easily cover a decent stretch of ground on the flat. With good chunky tyres, and both front and rear brakes the Strida seems a stable and safe alternative for those longer trips to the shops or main marina buildings.

The main frame is constructed from aluminium alloy tube with plastic injected mouldings, so should be maintenance- and corrosion-free even in a salty environment. The all-up weight is less than 22 lb (10 kg). The bike certainly has style of its own, is ergonomically sound, that is, easy for us mortals to use, and most important, functional.

Points for deliberation

- What is the Strida product concept?
- What are the key product attributes?
- At what particular customer group(s) might the product be aimed?
- What key customer needs are being met?
- What pricing strategy should Strida adopt?
- In view of the above points, how logical is Strida's intended distribution strategy?

Note

1 *Motorboats Monthly*, November 1987, 50.

Further reading

Fowler, A. and D. (1986) *Mail-Order – A Small Business Guide*, Sphere Reference.

Christopher, M. (1984) *The Strategy of Distribution Management*, London: Heinemann.

8 Marketing communications

Synopsis

Communication is the element of the marketing mix that covers the many forms of the firm's contact with existing customers or potential customers. It can be indirect, such as product packaging, mailshots, newspaper advertising, and word-of-mouth recommendation or direct, such as personal representation and point-of-sale contact. Each method of communication varies in the degree of influence it can exert on the customer and the choice and balance of methods used will depend on what objective needs to be achieved at a particular point in time. The objectives – which should be guided by the overall marketing strategy – may vary from simply making customers aware of something new to inducing the sale of the product or service.

Need for effective communication

Of all the elements of the marketing mix, communication with customers and other interest groups seems to be the least understood and probably the most abused. It cannot be stressed too strongly that communication in all its various forms provides the life-blood for sustaining a constant customer awareness of, and interest in, both the firm and its products. It is also the key to cementing customer loyalty and to developing conviction without which the firm will be that much more vulnerable to competitive activity.

We cannot simply assume that what the firm itself perceives as a good-quality product or competitive price or good after-sales service will induce purchase, for if these attributes are inadequately communicated to the customer the prospect of adoption becomes that much more chancy.

Marketing communications

Communication objectives

Communication, or promotion in its better known form, covers many activities most of which are indirect in approach. That is to say, they are non-personal forms of communication as opposed to personal, face-to-face contact with the customer. The latter is mainly associated with personal selling, where the communication of detailed product information or persuasion to try and to ultimately adopt the product, are generally the key objectives.

Non-personal forms of communication such as advertising, exhibitions, mailshots, press releases, etc., are really a means of 'drawing the horse to the water' and rarely will, in themselves, actually sell products. While there is no doubt that the ultimate objective will be to increase the level of business, communications strategy should recognize the need to fulfil various sub-objectives, which acknowledge both the anticipated behaviour of the customer and the effectiveness of the various methods of communication that are available. Additionally, any campaign should be linked to the overall desired marketing strategy and not be treated in isolation.

Developing a logical approach

Communications strategy should be seen as a continuation of the overall planning function, not only because it forms part of a logical development but also, because it provides for a system of checkpoints against which the firm can judge both the rationale behind, and ultimate effectiveness of, communication decisions.

This overall process is outlined in Figure 8.1 which represents the top-down approach to setting objectives and strategies. This hierarchical approach, while it may seem too highly formalized and mechanistic for the average small business, does provide a means of challenging the rationale behind decisions which are often based on personal intuition or on, say, some misguided tradition. Of course, it is hardly workable if the firm does not operate a formal system of planning but then again, it serves to illustrate the difficulties of making co-ordinated decisions in the absence of overall guidelines.

For example, if we were to consider decisions at the communications- or promotions-mix level, such as deciding on the balance between advertising, mailshots, exhibitions, leaflets, etc., we would need to consider what is to be achieved (objectives).

- Is it necessary to create awareness of the product or service?

Marketing in Small Businesses

- Do we wish to generate enquiries which need to be followed up by personal selling?
- Is the objective merely to remind customers of our existence?

Linkage with overall objectives

Without some guidance from specific marketing objectives it would be difficult to quantify communications objectives and thus, it is often a case of a 'shot in the dark'. Similarly, the absence of quantifiable business objective(s) will hinder the formulation and co-ordination of an effective marketing strategy.

The following simple flowchart serves to highlight the logical development:

1   Business objective   – Increase return on capital employed by 5 per cent pa.
    ↓

2   Marketing objective   – Increase present market share by 15 per cent of the current value.
    ↓

3   Communications objective   – Increase present customer enquiries by 50 per cent.

In this particular case, we would need to have some idea of how many enquiries on average result in orders, the current share of the market and, of course, what level and mix of communication would be needed to generate the extra enquiries. The latter is, however, not an easy task and it may be a case of experimenting over time. In the remainder of this chapter it is hoped to dispel some of these uncertainties by concentrating on some of the more useful concepts and techniques of communications strategy.

Thinking the problem through

In planning communications strategy, whatever the objectives might be, it is useful to think in terms of a general, simple model. Figure 8.2 is descriptive of most, if not all, communication situations where there is some message to be communicated to a target audience and through a particular channel of communication. For example, it could be the

Marketing communications

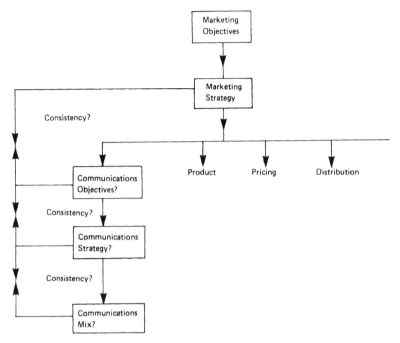

Figure 8.1 Developing communications strategy

announcement of a new product (message) to existing customers (target audience) via a mailshot (channel).

Target audience

In using the model, however, it is good practice to start from the target audience and work back towards the message, i.e. the reverse of the flow of communication, so that the message can be tailored to appeal to the target audience and appear in the appropriate media.

The start of the decision process must, of course, primarily be concerned with the overall objective(s) to be achieved, as discussed earlier. However, it should be borne in mind that any target audience in considering purchase of a product or service will normally go through a series of logical steps and any communication decisions should recognize this process. In fundamental terms the process is as follows:

1   Recognition of a need – internally or externally stimulated.
2   Search for information – the more expensive the product

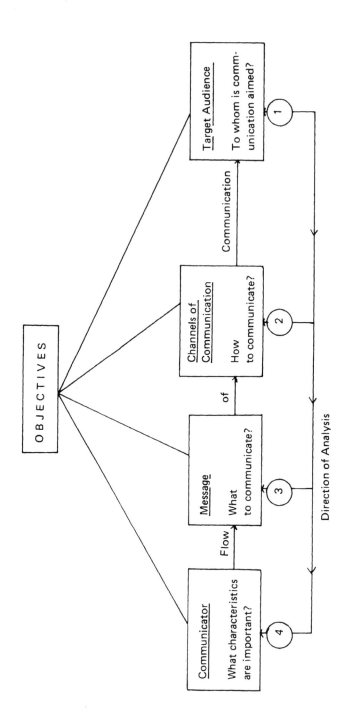

Figure 8.2 Simplified communications model

or service, the longer the search process.
3   Evaluation of available offerings – comparison of product and/or supplier features.
4   Selection, trial, and adoption (or rejection).

In communication terms the seller should develop and progressively implement a strategy which has at its base, a set of corresponding objectives; that is:

1   To create customer awareness of the product or service.
2   To impart sufficient information about the product or service.
3   To stimulate a liking and preference for the product or service.
4   To encourage purchase of the product or service.

It will be appreciated by the reader that as this process develops the more difficult it becomes to achieve the particular communications objective. Any campaign, of course, must be backed by a sound understanding of the needs and wants of the target audience and, better still, an understanding of their purchasing behaviour, media habits, and location.

Impact of buyer needs and behaviour

In some cases, it may be a problem deciding which particular target group we need to address. For example, in capital equipment selling the customer invariably comprises a decision-making team whose individuals, although aiming towards a central objective, will often have varying needs and different levels of influence in the buying process. As the latter is often a lengthy process the small business selling to the industrial sector may find it confusing as to *what* to communicate, to *whom*, *when* to communicate and *how* to communicate.

Sometimes, those who greatly influence the buying process may be external to the buying organization, such as outside consultants and thus, communicating direct with companies may sometimes have little or no effect on progress. The small business should try to identify whom to communicate with and what the overall needs are likely to be.

Purchasing in XY Chemical Company

The initial need is decided at HQ level and this is followed by consultations with the chief chemist and the process design engineer. Depending on the design effect required, the company may contact consultants or invite selected suppliers to offer preliminary solutions. Once the initial specification is drawn up requests for proposals are sent out to at least five approved suppliers. At this stage the chemist, process design engineer, plant engineer and buying department have been involved and during the evaluation of proposals the chief maintenance engineer is also consulted as accessibility to equipment is of vital importance in times of breakdown. The whole process can take anything from six to eighteen months and during this time those who influence the buying process express their own particular desires at varying stages of the evaluation procedure and up to the point of selection. For example:

> *Buyer*: 'As well as approving suppliers on the basis of capability and financial stability, I have to get the best quality/financial deal for the company.'
> *Process design engineer*: 'Equipment performance and design are high on the list of priorities.'
> *Chemist*: 'The quality and consistency of the ultimate proprietary product is obviously of paramount importance.'
> *Plant engineer*: 'Reliability means production efficiency and my performance is judged by this.'
> *Maintenance engineer*: 'I'm more concerned with how quickly the equipment can be pulled to pieces and reassembled.'

Although some of these individual needs overlap, the reader will appreciate that an effective communications strategy should recognize the composition of needs and the levels of individual influence in the purchasing process.

For consumer products and services target group identification is less of a problem although some deliberation is necessary with regard to purchasing behaviour. For example, the purchaser may not be the ultimate end-user, say, as in the case of many children's products which are bought by the mother or father, and the communicator must decide to whom the message should be directed, in order to have maximum impact. Similarly, both purchaser and end-user (if different) needs must be considered if the product or service benefits are to be properly communicated.

Regent Models

The Jackson brothers, with several years of construction engineering behind them, hit on the idea of a building model which could be used in schools and colleges as teaching/occupational aids. They had spent several months developing the idea and eventually ended up with a series of products in kit form. Following a simple plan, the models could be built up from basic wooden components using a simple gluing process, which virtually simulated the real thing. A major distributor was contacted and, following negotiations, the product was included in their mail-order catalogue. The partners had tested the idea with a school-teacher colleague and were satisfied that the orders would roll in, but when they attempted to obtain external funding for the venture, some doubts were raised.

Eventually, it transpired that a major criticism was the inability to re-use the kit because of the need to glue the components together and, in view of the basic cost of the kit, many local authority purchasing organizations might consider it cost-ineffective because of its inability to be re-used.

Conclusion

What seemed a bright and innovative idea thus turned into disappointment and possibly wasted effort. Although the partners had an effective channel of communication (through the distributor's catalogue) and had considered the potential end-user needs in a deliberate manner, they had overlooked one important element. Had they considered the needs of the key influencer in the buying process, they might well have given more thought to the assembly method.

Channels of communication

Interpersonal communication

Although there are several ways in which the small firm may 'reach' its end-users and/or intermediaries, rarely will a sale be made without some fact-to-face personal influence. The degree of personal influence required to induce purchase will, to some extent, depend upon the nature of the product and its cost.

With high-priced products, and particularly where risk is involved, the buyer will generally seek more information than that communicated by advertising, publicity material, etc. It may simply be a matter of the salesman, say, arranging a product demonstration or discussing after-sales service, but sometimes the buyer may turn to third-party sources for reassurance and conviction. 'Social channels' of communication can be very influential in this respect, such as a

Marketing in Small Businesses

personal recommendation from a friend or a trusted business acquaintance. Similarly, the buyer may turn to outside professional experts as in the case of the 'XY Chemical Company' discussed previously. Perhaps to stress the point the reader will more readily relate to the following comments:

Housewife: 'My husband and I had virtually made up our minds about the new fitted kitchen when a casual remark about the supplier's poor reputation for fitting was overheard by my husband at his club. Needless to say, we started to look around again.'

Purchasing manager: 'I knew the supplier had installed similar equipment at Company Y so I rang the buyer there and he confirmed the company's claims.'

Teenager: 'My friend, Janice, was telling me about the holiday she'd had in Mallorca and how helpful the travel agent had been – I just went down and booked there and then.'

Managing director: 'When I look back, I'm sure I realized the product was good, but the way the salesman put over the presentation just seemed to lack any conviction and I could see other members of the board sinking deeper into their seats.'

Some business theorists would argue that this interpersonal influence is so strong that the seller would do better devoting most of his promotional effort towards satisfying existing customers. This assumes that if the customers are continuously reassured and properly serviced then the wider market is more likely to adopt, given time. It is also widely held that certain groups of consumers are classed as 'opinion leaders' and that if the firm is lucky enough to gain their attention they can be very influential in persuading other consumers to buy the product or service.

However, it is not always easy to identify and locate these so-called key-influencers, but it could be assumed that some would more readily adopt a new product or idea and thus be regarded as trend setters. This is clearly the case for 'fashionable' products as we have seen with the mass imitators of Princess Diana, be it hairstyle or dress, and pop fans' identification with particular groups in their purchasing and other behaviours.

While it may be impracticable for the small firm to research into these factors of interpersonal and leadership communication behaviours, a recognition of their existence should help in formulating communications strategy and making the best use of limited budgets. If promotion activity and selling effort is largely devoted to gaining

Marketing communications

new customers, then the possible impact on existing customers should be a point for deliberation. We can never be sure just how much interpersonal communication is at play or how influential it may be, but we can be sure that it exists in most, of not all, situations.

Advertising

Non-personal channels of communication cover the remaining promotional techniques such as media advertising, direct mail, publicity, promotional offers, and packaging. Each has its own part to play, such as creating awareness, imparting information, stimulating interest or encouraging enquiries for further information. For the small firm, denied the more lavish media of, say, television and bill posters, the choice of promotional mix is very much limited and, therefore, extra care is needed in making the most of a limited budget. Each method must be treated on its merits and viewed in light of the objectives to be achieved.

Fundamentally, advertising works to make potential buyers (and, indeed, existing customers) respond more favourably to the company and its products or services. It is a means of communicating information and creating desire for further information, or for the product, but its overall effectiveness is contentious, to say the least. It is often difficult to measure its effectiveness except in cases where it calls for a *direct* response from the potential buyer to the communicating company, such as in mail-order advertising where the level of orders through different publications can be monitored, or where a trade journal advertisement invites enquiries from its readers through means of a reply slip. None the less, it will be appreciated that the method is widely practised by both large and small companies alike, if not always with a proper sense of direction.

Advertising, as any other method of communication, should be seen as part of the overall marketing strategy and, therefore, it should be goal-orientated. Likewise, its limitations should be recognized and, of course, good advertising will not compensate for inferior products or services. Generally, advertising will be greater in effectiveness when:

- Customer awareness of the product and/or the company is low.
- The product or service being advertised is heavily differentiated from its competitors, or it is new.
- The overall market for the product or service is buoyant and not stagnant or declining.

However, certain writers contend that advertising plays little part in persuading potential customers or at least, that it doesn't have the 'brainwashing' power that is often attributed to this method of communication. Unlike in personal selling, the target audience may miss, or can elect to ignore the message, particularly if it is one of many appearing in the same medium. For example, with print media, the reader tends to be selective both in choice of publication and in focusing attention on the contents therein.

Commercial television, of course, commands a greater reach and is generally more effective at attracting and holding attention. The audio-visual flexibility is ideal for products that need to be demonstrated in order to highlight the benefits and, in some cases, the ads can be more interesting than the adjacent programmes. Until, however, advertising costs are reduced significantly, the average small firm must be content with the run-of-the-mill media.

What must be borne in mind is that advertising should be seen as a 'building up' process and not as an instantaneous-response mechanism. There are thus both time and exposure factors involved, leading to a desired level of reach to, and response from, the target audience. Even where it may seem to demand an immediate sales response without personal intervention, such as in mail-order advertising, we cannot say for sure just how many separate advertisements a particular customer was exposed to before taking action. Unless the firm is blessed with a revolutionary product or service, it will take more than the odd advertisement to gain an adequate level of response.

Message design and the communicator

Certainly, good advertising can be used to build familiarity, act as a reminder or generate interest, and this depends to a large extent on what the communicating company has to say and how this is presented to, and interpreted by, the observer.

Not only is it important to understand the behaviour and needs of the target audience, but the communicator must also have some idea of the state of the audience – such as their current level of faith in, and familiarity with, the company and its products. As the audience needs to be taken through a series of steps towards the ultimate purchasing action, no one message is likely to induce the level of credibility required. For example, we first need to make the audience aware, then it becomes necessary to stimulate their interest followed by a desire to try the product or service.

Additionally, the use of personal and non-personal channels of communication must be co-ordinated and timed to produce maximum impact, otherwise scarce resources may be wasted. For example, if the level of awareness of the company and its products is low, personal selling will be that much harder. Of course, it is probably true that many small businesses rely solely on personal selling and do so quite successfully. However, if it is felt that there is a need to advertise, then this is better carried out in a co-ordinated manner.

Designing the message

In designing the message, creativity must be guided by an appreciation of the target audience needs and the particular objectives to be achieved. Rather than flood the receiver's mind with a mass of information about the company and its products it is much more effective to concentrate on one or two key features which have a bearing on the communication objectives and the receiver's existing level of awareness and needs. Too many simultaneous claims will generally lack credibility in the mind of the receiver and, thus, the impatient firm may do more harm than good in trying to accelerate the buying process unduly by bombarding the potential customer with too much information at any one time.

Similarly, the choice of channel of communication will, to some extent, affect the message design and format. For example, in a personal selling role the communicator has the opportunity to vary the message according to customer response at the particular time and imparting information in a 'real-time' situation (e.g. immediately responding to questions from the customer). Denied this flexibility in, say, newspaper advertising or mailshots, the communicating company must decide on what balance of information and message format is needed to maximize the effect of a small budget.

Argus Software

Alan Smithson had set up in partnership in 1984, with Ron Jackson, to offer customized business computer software to local industry. Both partners were experienced computer programmers, having worked for a well-known computer manufacturer for several years.

The decision to go on their own had been stimulated by what they saw as a rapidly expanding market brought about by the ever-decreasing cost of computer hardware.

In the early days of formation, the company had managed to win over a small number of customers from their previous company. However, the partners were more interested in developing the small-business market where personal computers were increasingly being adopted.

Marketing in Small Businesses

They not only offered software services to existing computer users, but also 'turnkey' services to potential users. That is, they would take over the complete task of assessing requirements, specifying computer hardware, designing the software, installing the system, offering training and continuous service arrangements.

The partners had (rightly) acknowledged that a heavy reliance would be needed on personal selling and that they would first need to generate a fair volume of enquiries. Fortunately, the company had managed to get a press release in the local newspaper and although no enquiries had resulted from this, the partners felt confident that there was some level of awareness among the target audience. Several weeks later, they placed an advertisement in the same newspaper which basically described the services on offer. Essentially, the features emphasized were:

- Customized software.
- Range of computer languages.
- Range of business systems covered.
- Hardware specifications.

When it was eventually realized that the advertisement had proved ineffective, the company decided on a mailshot to local firms. A leaflet designed much on the above lines, and a covering letter, were sent out (addressed to 'the managing director') to about a hundred small/medium-sized companies. This eventually resulted in a half-a-dozen or so enquiries of which one eventually turned into an order for a 'specialized' stock control programme.

Some twelve months after start-up, the company had not generated sufficient business to cover costs and had reached a point where the future seemed very uncertain. Ron Jackson commented: 'I just don't understand it. We offer a first-class service and there are so many high-street "cowboys" about (referring to certain computer retail outlets). Just the other day I lost out to a rival company who only provide standard systems. I felt sure the customer was on our side after explaining in detail the hardware specification and the advantages of using the PC DOS operation system. What do we have to do to get the business?'

Conclusion

It seems that, accepting there would also be intense competitive forces at play, Argus were misreading the real customer needs and as such their 'message design', in not highlighting the real customer benefits, was ill-conceived. We can never be sure without a detailed analysis, why the business was failing to take-off, but poor communication would not help the situation. The average customer would probably not understand the hardware or software implications, let alone be stimulated to seek further information or to place an order. His real needs would be focused on the business in terms of increased efficiency and cost-effectiveness and, in some cases, the impact on certain employees.

It is essential to try to understand what goes on in the buyer's mind at the various stages of the purchasing process, especially in the closing stages, for here the risks involved come much more to the surface. The ultimate message not only has to convince but also has to provide reassurance and for the more complex, high-value products and services, the onus will be on the communicator to ensure that the message is matched to these objectives.

Where purchasing is stimulated totally through non-personal channels such as mail-order advertising, it should be recognized that there is also a greater, perceived risk on the part of the customer. Thus it is more often than not necessary to provide reassurance say, in the form of a 'money-back guarantee' statement or a 'trail period' offer.

Communicator characteristics

Whether communicating personally or non-personally, the recipient individual will form an opinion about the communicating company. Salesmen have often been labelled the 'ambassadors of the company' and if the customer has a low level of awareness of the particular company, he or she will very likely base an opinion on the qualities of the representative. Likewise, with non-personal forms of communication such as advertising, initial opinions of the company can only really be formed on the basis of the source, presentation and content of the message.

Considerable research has been carried out into the social and psychological factors surrounding these perceptions, much of it, of course, beyond the scope of this text. However, there are certain commonly agreed factors which can be expressed in readily understandable terms and which can be of use in planning communications strategy. These are customers' perceptions of:

- The company's general trustworthiness.

Marketing in Small Businesses

- The company's competence in the particular line of business.
- The company's ability to sustain its position, e.g. its resource base and standing in the market.

There is an additional factor which is perhaps more relevant to consumer markets and that is concerned with customers' perception of the 'friendliness' of the communicating company (or its representatives).

In planning communications strategy, attention should be paid to all of these factors in order to promote the best possible image. At least, advertising campaigns, publicity material and personal selling style, etc. should be scrutinized to guard against any possible negative attitudes arising on the part of the target audience. A perceived weakness in any one characteristic is likely to affect the overall company image and thus reduce its credibility as a business entity.

It is useful to think broadly in terms of communication activity as an invitation to form a long-term association as far as potential customers are concerned and as a means of continuous reassurance in terms of existing customers. In each case, evidence of trustworthiness, capability and long-term survival potential will help to stimulate trial and adoption and lay the foundation for establishing customer loyalty.

The following comments will serve to highlight the impact of inattention to some of the characteristics discussed:

Buyer: 'I received the product literature through the post and first impressions were not encouraging. The material was obviously photocopied and not too good at that. Although the company were claiming high product quality, I couldn't help thinking that if this was anything to go by they'd be lucky to qualify as second-rate.' (resources/capability?)

Financial director: 'The rep was a nice chap, but he didn't seem to know much about the system. Whenever I asked a pointed question he would just say that he would get the information from someone else in the company.' (expertness?)

Housewife: 'When I saw the advertisement announcing the opening of the new restaurant, it just seemed uninviting. We had thought of going there for our anniversary but driving all that way just out of curiosity seemed a bit of a risk. The menu looked fine on paper, but you really need a good atmosphere and services as well.' (likeability/friendliness?)

Newly married couple: 'We rang the shop every week and it was always the same old story. If the sales assistant had told us in the first place that delivery would have taken so long we could have

Marketing communications

made temporary arrangements. How can you rely on a company that cons you into buying?' (trustworthiness?)

The key to effective communication is ensuring that there is a positive mix of the above characteristics whatever the channel of contact.

Creating a favourable image will obviously have its resource implications, but it should not be beyond the small company to stick to the basic guidelines. Before dismissing any decision on the basis of cost, evaluate the possible consequences of choosing cheaper alternatives and bear in mind that whatever you think about your own organization, customers can only judge by what they see and experience.

Communications planning

The following case illustrates the role of communications strategy within the overall marketing plan.

Morrison's (Meats) Ltd

Morrison's was established at the turn of the century as a family butchers and in 1985 the company comprised four retail shops along with pies and cooked meat manufacturing. The latter business served several retail grocers in the area operating on a van/sales basis.

In 1986 the owner, Arthur Morrison, decided to capitalize on the growth in pub catering. He had the idea of producing ready-to-cook, frozen meat-based dishes which could be enhanced by a range of English and Continental sauces. At the same time, he decided to sell off the butchers shops which were the least profitable of his business activities.

He was firmly convinced that the new products would sell but, wisely, he commissioned a preliminary market study which was carried out by staff from the local college's catering studies department (partly funded under the Department of Industry's Business Improvement Services scheme – BIS).

Basic desk research confirmed the national growth in pub catering and a field survey among a sample of pubs (60) within a 15-mile radius indicated that some 5 per cent of the target market would be very keen to follow up the new product ideas. The survey also established: the key decision-makers with regard to purchasing supplies and setting menus and their 'needs'; what trade journals were received and actually read, current suppliers, number of meals served in a week and price indications (of

143

Marketing in Small Businesses

course, not all respondents were prepared to give 100 per cent information and this must never be taken for granted in any survey of this nature!).

When product development was nearing completion the researchers, in conjunction with the college's department of business studies, set about advising on the new product launch and the following plan was agreed in consultation with Arthur Morrison.

New product plan

Product

Range of high quality, frozen meat dishes with various sauces, in individual and multiple packs.

Target market

Tenanted, managed and freehouse pubs within a 15-mile radius.

Marketing objectives

To achieve 2 per cent share by end of first year and to increase this by a further 3 per cent at end of year 2.

Marketing strategy

Secure adoption initially by 'innovators', then further gradual penetration consistent with build up of demand and production capacity.

Communications strategy

Selective and continuous communication with main concentration in first half of year.

Creative strategy

Publicity leaflets
- Message to stress 'new' development and 'quality' of product range.
- Highlight company's long-established business in quality provisions.
- Covering letter to be produced on word processor to give a 'personalized' presentation.

Journal advertisement (*Catering*)
- To complement mailshot and subsequent telephone calls – enhance acceptance.

Marketing communications

- To expose company name and established business.
- To provide talking point during sales calls.

Personal selling
- Stress convenience of preparation.
- Stress low waste factor.
- Stress prompt delivery, particularly at short notice.

Demonstration
- Stress flexibility in preparation – use both traditional oven and microwave methods.
- Prepare full product range for taste tests.
- Stress benefits compared with competitive offerings.

Journal advertisement (*Inn Keeper*)
- Stress acceptance by test market, particularly of most popular items.
- Reiterate existing, established business.
- Provide a balance of 'innovativeness' and 'traditional quality service' themes.

Conclusion

It may be thought that the initial promotional costs (see Figure 8.3) were rather high as indeed did Arthur Morrison, having just paid for the market study. He had now begun to realize however, the need for a logical and systematic approach to the problem. He now appreciated that:

- Only a small percentage of pubs would be adventurous enough to innovate in the early stages of market development.
- The large majority of pubs would be reluctant to change the status quo with regard to catering (in the early stages at least).
- There was a need to concentrate promotional expenditure rather than spread it thinly over the year.
- If he was reluctant to spend the recommended amount on communication, then the pre-determined marketing objectives would have to be revised.

Whatever the size of the communication task or the objectives to be achieved, it is worth thinking the issues through in a systematic fashion. Not only is it likely to lead to more effective targetting but also, it will generally mean more efficient use of resources. Any significant imbalance between use of direct and indirect forms of communication and particularly the timing of such, is more likely to result in waste of resources and loss of confidence in the relevant channels of communication.

Objectives / Channel	Create Awareness	Stimulate Interest	Stimulate Desire	Encourage Trial and Adoption	Reassure
"Inn Keeper" Journal					¼ page insert
Telephone		Follow up selection of non-responders to mail-shot			
"Catering" Journal	¼ page insert				
Mail-Shot	1,000 leaflets and covering letters				
Sales Calls		Deal with responses (Approx.40 calls @ ½ hour each)			
Demonstration			By invitation, College Catering School (30 heads approx)		
Sample Offers				Approx 30 mixed packs (at cost)	
Budget	£880.00	£200.00	£220.00	£180.00	£340.00
Week No.	1 2 3 4	5 6 7 8 9	10 11 12 13 13	15 16 17	18 – 25

Total Budget (6 months) = £1,820

Figure 8.3 Promotion/communications schedule and budget (new product launch)

Marketing communications

Checklist

- How effective are the firm's present methods of communicating?
- How many potential customers are reachable with the present methods?
- What are the customer needs/wants with regard to the particular product/service?
- What are their media habits?
- What is the current level of awareness regarding the company and product/services?
- Can the benefits of the product/service be communicated effectively through the usual media?
- How cost-effective is the media in question?
- Do other forms of communication such as exhibitions, personal selling, mailshots, need to be considered?
- Does what is communicated about the product/service, match the benefits the customer is seeking?
- In what way can the communication methods used be measured for effectiveness?
- Do the methods and media in use reflect favourably on both the product/service and the company?

Case study: W. Jordan (Cereals)[1]

The combination of oats, raw sugar, bran, seeds, and raisins that makes up granola has turned the millers – the Jordan family – into one of the health market's success stories. It prompted the division of the original family firm, W. Jordan and Sons, into two companies, to cope with its traditional animal feeds business and the burgeoning branded foods operation. In the late 1960s, Jordan's animal feed products, supplemented by some production of own-label white flours, just about kept the company's head above water. But it looked as if the mill might go the way of the rest of Bedfordshire's independent mills: either into the clutches of a milling giant, or simply into dereliction.

Over a decade later, when W. Jordan (Cereals) was formed in the early 1980s, the company had footholds in two important growth markets: granola cereal and cereal bars, backed up by healthy sales in such other wholefood sectors as wholewheat flours, bran, wheatgerm and standard mueslis.

Reproduced by kind permission of W. Jordan (Cereals) Ltd.

Marketing communications

The £4 million turnover of 1980 grew to £13 million in 1985, an annual gain of at least 30 per cent per annum – and Jordan's major markets continued to expand. The Jordans still run their original mill, but the old building, set on a tree-lined river bank, is now juxtaposed with a much more recent extension built to churn out enough granola to satisfy 40 per cent of the granola cereal market, and nearly a third of bar sales.

Now the UK's largest independent millers, Jordan's has not won its success easily, and it is still locked in a ferocious battle for market share with other manufacturers following the granola route. It's a situation that is unlikely to change. 1985 brought new developments in the bar market from competitive camps and the US-inspired 'soft' bars were poised to hit grocery shelves with the backing of General Mills. Instead of playing the giants at their own game, however, Jordans plotted a course which underlined its original advantages in the health food market. Managing director Bill Jordan was instrumental in setting up, with other concerned parties, the Guild of Conservation Food Producers. The body restricts its farming members to the cultivation of crops grown by certain narrowly defined methods, which substantially cut down the number of pesticides and inorganic chemicals used in standard farming practice. The result is food untainted by synthetic chemicals – a benefit Jordan will make much of in its future development plans.

It pays a premium of 8 per cent for Conservation Grade grain, but this gives Jordan's the point of difference from the commercial giants now muscling in on its markets. Granola bars clock up over £50 million worth of sales annually, and growth is good enough to catch the eye of the big boys. Jordan's refuses to let its brand disappear amid the welter of heavily supported household names, and believes the consumer is on its side in the move towards purer foods.

As the pioneer of the granola market in the UK, Jordan's has had to fight hard for both distribution and consumer credibility. It was not a name familiar to national accounts in the early 1970s and, while granola answered a need in the newly active health food sector, it did so indirectly. Many people simply did not know what to do with the product. 'They were a bit nonplussed by granola cereal when it first appeared,' admits managing director Bill Jordan. 'In those days, people thought it was either bird food or Alpen.'

American idea

Jordan, who is in his late thirties, brought the idea of granola back from a trip to the US in the late 1960s. At the time he was not consciously trawling for new ideas, he says; it was more that the prospect of

Marketing in Small Businesses

immersing himself in the animal feedstuffs business for the rest of his working life didn't exactly fire his imagination.

'At the time, we were manufacturing flour too, but it was white flour, and the goods were being sold under supermarkets' own-labels. This was crazy. We had a unique flour mill – but the only market was for white flour. The only brand in an almost non-existent wholemeal sector was Allinson.'

The nutritionally naïve British, it seemed, were getting a worse deal than the animals they fattened. 'All the good parts of our raw materials were ending up in the animal feeds,' Jordan adds.

At the beginning of the 1970s, the Jordan family decided to take a risk and switch flour production to wholemeal. The products were to be sold under its own name. The bread-and-butter own-label business, meanwhile, became puffed wheat and rice cereal manufacture. Bill Jordan joined his father's business as sales and marketing director – a position he retained until the Cereals firm was set up in 1981, with himself as managing director. 'I did literally all the marketing until three years ago,' he says, 'and until 1976 I did all the selling too.' The new firm gained a marketing manager soon after its formation, in response to competitive pressures and the need to pull together a forceful advertising campaign. Graham Lee, who joined the company in 1984, is the second incumbent in this position.

W. Jordan (Cereals) now employs some 180 staff, and the family complement includes Bill Jordan's brother, David, as technical director and sister, Lindsay Frost, who oversees research and development. In the early 1970s Bill Jordan was faced with carving out distribution for the wholemeal flours range from scratch. His problems were doubled by the health food trade's fragmentation. Until Booker McConnell's health products division pulled together its Holland and Barrett chain towards the middle of the decade and began to chivvy the independents retailing was highly unstructured.

The mechanics of distribution, too, were far from simple. 'One of the inherent problems with wholefoods,' says Jordan, 'is that you use ingredients which aren't stabilized and so are more perishable by nature than further treated foods.' He got round the obstacle by buying van space from fruit importer Geest, which delivered in most high streets. By dint of sheer hard selling, the brand began to make an impression on the independents' health retail market. It soon caught the eye of Booker, which controlled the UK's biggest health food products wholesaler, Brewhurt, and eventually gained a listing. This secured coverage of the specialist health retail trade for its three flours and two milling by-products – bran and wheatgerm.

Unwritten rule

By then, the trend towards healthier food was gathering momentum, and Jordan's ploughed its resources into product development, with the unwritten rule that future product launches should not duplicate products already on the market. Tests on granola began in 1973, when a pilot plant to produce the cereal mix was built. 'We spent some time working on that, adjusting the recipe to get it right,' says Jordan.

Weetabix, meanwhile, was doing much to open up the muesli market with Alpen. Jordan admits that he is indebted to the cereal giant for diligently supporting its brand at a time when the public needed a lot of persuasion to pour what looked to them much like cat litter into their cereal bowls. Jordan's Original Crunchy cereal needed a hefty sampling programme to support its launch, however, and for the first few years had to go it alone in the granola cereal market. The company's big break came when the Waitrose chain gave its brand a listing in 1976, bringing with it a new respectability. Once Jordan's moved into the multiple trade, it was inevitable that competitors would begin to line up.

Towards the end of the decade, Quaker Oats rolled out its Harvest Crunch granola cereal, with the full weight of the Quaker distribution franchise and publicity machine behind it. It helped to build the market, but the Quaker brand also jumped in, on the back of its sister cereal products, where Jordan's coverage was not yet strong: in the multiple grocery sector. 'We were very nervous about moves like this,' admits Jordan. 'But we always had the full support of the entire health foods trade and we still tend to regard our strength as being in this area, although it now accounts for only 40 per cent of total distribution.'

Research into the usage of Original Crunchy confirmed that the UK market was heading in the same direction as its counterpart in the US. 'It showed that 30 per cent of purchasers had eaten it as a snack, rather than as a conventional breakfast cereal,' explains Jordan. 'We took the basic granola bar concept and anglicized it quite heavily. For British tastes, you need a much higher proportion of the more expensive ingredients – nuts and fruit – and less sugar.' Original Crunchy bars began to flow on to the store shelves in 1980 and were closely followed by Quaker's Harvest Crunch bars. There is no love lost between the two companies in the granola bar sector, and Jordan had his work cut out to persuade multiple retailers that the more specialist Original Crunchy brand merited a listing – at least as well as the more confectionery-orientated Quaker line.

Marketing manager Lee is pleased that Quaker has stuck to its original positioning. 'Fortunately for us,' he says, 'they took the

Marketing in Small Businesses

shorter route to the children's sector, with smaller, sweeter bars. We leaned towards adults, an area which we think has the greatest long-term potential. We'd seen people get interested in granola cereals for health reasons, after all, and Quaker seemed to ignore this.' Lee points out that Original Crunchy bars, like the cereal, have no artificial additives and are relatively low in sugar, but high in fibre, while the fats they contain are polyunsaturated. 'These product claims are totally consistent with the National Advertising Committee of Nutrition Education and the Committee of Medical Aspects of Food Policy recommendations,' he says, adding that 'you only have to study the packs of our competitors to see that they have tried to mask high sugar levels, by listing several different types of sugar.' Quaker's muscle in the multiple grocery trade gave its brand the edge. The relative brand shares of Original Crunchy and Harvest Crunch are a subject on which the two manufacturers seem destined never to agree. The granola cereal market was worth £11 million in 1983. Over the next three years brand leadership changed hands several times with both brands each consistently holding over 30 per cent of the market. The situation is more complex where granola bars are concerned. This market, worth £52 million in 1987, shot up by 44 per cent during 1985 – a growth level not expected to slow up in the short term. According to Jordan's, Quaker's smaller, cheaper Harvest Crunch bars account for 30 per cent of sales by volume, compared with Jordan's 15 per cent share. Natural Crunch, from Fox's Biscuits – which once retailed under Weetabix's Alpen brand – takes just 5 per cent of volume sales. If shares are measured in sterling terms, however, the gap between the two main protagonists narrows significantly; Jordan's claims 18 per cent against Quaker's 20 per cent.

A host of smaller brands and own-label lines make up the remaining granola sales. The big US and UK biscuit, confectionery, and cereal manufacturers, which might have been expected to have swooped early and cleaned up on the novelty value of granola bars – if the production process were not so specialized – have launched a string of products since 1985. United Biscuits' Solar bar went into a test market in 1984, and in autumn 1985 BN Biscuits and Foods, the UK arm of General Foods, launched a 'second-generation' soft granola bar under the Jump brand. Since then Allied-Lyons have launched Cluster (chewy & crunchy variants), Mars have launched Tracker (soft confectionery layered bar), Rowntree Mackintosh 'Naro' (a chocolate-coated soft cereal bar), and Cadbury's 'Go' (also chocolate-coated).

Reviving flagging sales

General Mills is adamant that the UK market is ripe for the advent of the soft bar, which revived flagging sales in the US. But Jordan believes that this development loses sight of granola's original appeal. 'In the US,' he says, 'the market went full circle very quickly. In no time at all, the very big names became involved and dosed the products with sugar. The initial claims were lost, and the sector lost both direction and credibility.'

Nevertheless, Jordan's defences are going up. Production is currently split 40:40:20 between cereals, bars, and flours, so it is relatively vulnerable, although its cereals business includes traditional mueslis. In the past two years, the Original Crunchy products have gained impetus from new flavour introductions – bran and apple, and honey and almond – and consumer advertising has emphasized Jordan's ethically correct positioning.

The first salvo was fired by TBWA in 1983. The agency devised a highly informative press and poster campaign, which set out to explain the difference between Jordan's ingredients and manufacturing methods and those of some other 'healthy' food manufacturers. The ad team left TBWA a year later to set up their own shop, Edward Martin Thornton, and the account went with them. In 1984 'people maintenance' push pressed home the health message. In 1985, the £300,000 account took new direction, 'because of the rate of change in people's attitudes,' according to Lee.

At Jordan's Mill, new capacity is constantly being added to satisfy demand. Such investment cripples profits – which Jordan is loath to discuss – but it means, at least, that the plant installed is state-of-the-art, which helps cost efficiency. Some £10 million has been ploughed into new machinery over the past six years.

The Conservation Grade issue should further widen the chasm between 'commercial' health foods, which often sport high sugar levels and additives, and the type of products Jordan's produce. So far, Jordan's seem to have fallen foul of no one: not the consumer, not the retailer, not even the medical profession, with its low-fat, high-fibre creed. The company's future strategy looks resilient. 'Over the next couple of years,' says Jordan, 'we don't see ourselves going very far outside this area. We have specialist knowledge of it, and we don't want to dilute that by branching out too far, too quickly or diversifying into something completely new.'

Points for deliberation

- What is Jordan's product concept?
- What is the nature of competition in this market?
- What is the market growth for granola bars?
- What were the earlier problems in distribution?

Marketing in Small Businesses

- To whom is the Jordan granola bar targeted and what is its positioning?
- What channels of communication have Jordan's used so far, according to the case?
- What is, or is likely to be, a key ingredient of message design?

Note

1 Extracted from Catherine Bond, 'Jordan's charts healthy course', *Marketing*, 25 April 1985, 23–7, and company sources.

Further reading

White, R. (1980) *Advertising. What it is and How to Do It*, Maidenhead: McGraw-Hill.

Tack, A. (1980) *How to Increase Your Sales to Industry*, Tadsworth: World's Work.

9 Overseas marketing

Synopsis

Exporting is regarded as the most basic form of international business activity. At the other extreme, the firm may elect to invest in manufacturing plant and marketing facilities within the host nation, although this is beyond the means of most small businesses. Indirect exporting involves the simple shipping of products abroad through export houses, to be handled ultimately by selected agents in the host countries. Direct exporting usually involves the firm in more of the overseas activity, such as the setting up of an export department and, possibly, an overseas sales branch. Each method has differing implications for risk, marketing costs, and marketing controls. Whatever methods are employed, it is generally recognized that some modification to the marketing mix, however small, will be necessary and that pre-empting such changes, through systematic research, will reduce the risk of failure.

The overseas marketing decision

For some small businesses the idea of exporting may hardly be a consideration, due to the nature and local or regional concentration of the business. Many small business activities, however, are capable of exploiting overseas opportunities, given the right sort of approach and the element of luck on which ultimate success often relies.

The conceptual approach to international marketing stresses the need for systematic planning, starting from a conscious decision to expand into international markets, through to reorganizing the firm to cope with the additional activities.

The process outlined in Figure 9.1 is a much simplified version of the conceptual approach and, in reality, it represents a complex, often costly and lengthy process which many small firms would find daunting. At the extreme, stages 2, 3 and 4 generally require extensive

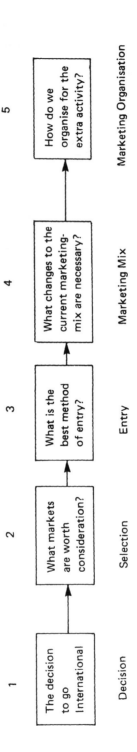

Figure 9.1 International marketing process

research in order to arrive at the various decision points. For example, stage 2 would normally involve the assessment of more than one possible market with a view to determining:

- *Relative degree of accessibility*: tariff barriers; non-tariff barriers.
- *Market attractiveness*: market size; per capita income expenditure; economic growth; extent of competition; product fit; political stability, etc.

Although much of this information is readily available from published sources such as government statistics and trade journals, it may be necessary to resort to original research in order to complete the picture; for example, detailed information on potential competitors and potential customers, which is generally an expensive commodity.

On a more practical level, a chance contact through an exhibition or, say, an enquiry from a specific overseas company, may at least reduce the problem to an analysis of a single host country. Alternatively, the contacting of an appropriate export agency may lead to a viable opportunity with the minimum of prior research. However, it is in the best interests of the firm to apply as much pre-planning as it deems feasible and within the constraints of available resources. There is no one easy way to develop overseas markets successfully.

Sources of information

As we have seen with domestic marketing in the earlier chapters, the various activities covered almost always require information in one form or another, followed by some pre-deliberation before taking action. The problems of overseas marketing are no different in nature, they are simply multiplied due to the inherent difficulties of gathering appropriate information, coping with differing market needs and managing the uncertainty that comes with a greater physical remoteness from the markets served.

The extent to which this uncertainty can be reduced depends to a large extent on how much time and effort the firm is prepared to spend on gathering and sifting through information. Where existing secondary sources of data prove inadequate (such as those listed in Table 9.1), the firm may elect to arrange for primary research to be carried out by a professional agency. Although the latter is relatively expensive, in some cases assistance may be obtained from the British Overseas Trade Board (BOTB) and the Department of Trade and Industry (DTI).

Marketing in Small Businesses

Useful sources of published international market data
- British Overseas Trade Board (regional).
- Chambers of Commerce (local).
- City Business Library (London).
- Department of Trade and Industry (regional).
- Department of Industry Statistics and Market Intelligence Library (London).
- Foreign embassies.
- National Economic Development Council (London).
- Organization for Economic Co-operation and Development.
- Overseas Industry Statistics (DTI booklet: *National Statistical Offices of Overseas Countries*).
- *World Sources of Market Information*, Gower Publishing Co.

As a general rule of thumb, secondary data sources should be thoroughly scrutinized before embarking on primary research, as the market information sought may already be in existence. For example, market reports relative to specific product areas can sometimes be purchased from UK and overseas research agencies for well below the cost of commissioned research (Table 9.1).

Market selection

If the overseas marketing decision is part of a deliberate planned strategy, ultimate market selection will be influenced by the comparative levels of market attractiveness and the perceived strengths of the firm in terms of product fit, competitiveness, and accessibility to the markets under review. Where the market selection decision is predetermined, say from a chance contact with a potential overseas client, it would of course, still pay to get as much background on the host market as possible.

Mode of entry

In each of the above cases, the method of entry will depend upon a number of factors, including: financial risks; the nature of the products or services in question; the level of pre-sales technical support and after-sales service required; the ability of the firm and/or competent agents or distributors to provide the latter; the distribution infrastructure within the host nation (if appropriate to the product or service); the level of resources which the firm is able to commit to the exporting function and the degree of marketing control that the firm is willing to accede.

Overseas marketing

Table 9.1 Examples of specific market reports and sources

Company/association	Report details	Price
Avia Chem Marketing Ltd 1 Court Downs Road Beckenham Kent 01-658 6610	Markets in W Europe: Acrylics into the 1980s	£100
Chemical Data Services Room CP 322 Dorset House Stamford Street London SE1 9LU 01-261 8609	Chemical Company Profiles: Western Europe Survey of 1,700 Pharmaceutical Companies	£40
Economist Intelligence Unit Spencer House 27 St James's Place London SW1A 1NT 01-493 6711	Marketing in Europe in-depth study of consumer markets in Western Europe, including food, drink, clothing, furniture and leisure goods	£155
Euromonitor Publications Ltd PO Box 115 41 Russell Square London WC1B 5DL 01-637 9517	European Marketing Data and Statistics Statistic on social, economic, and consumer topics with forecasts	£45
Frost and Sullivan Inc 104–112 Marylebone Lane London W1M 5FU 01-486 8377	Disinfectants and Sanitizers Markets in Europe Data on: products, end-uses, structure of the market; market forecasts	US $1,200
Furniture Industry Research Association Maxwell Road Stevenage Herts SG1 2EW 0438 313433	German Survey Information on prices and markets for specific products in the furniture industry	£95
German Chamber of Industry and Commerce 12/13 Suffolk Street St James's London SW1Y 4HG 01-930 7251	Freight forwarding market in West Germany	£69
O.A. Goulden and Partners Quarry House Stoke Hill Stoke Andover Hants 0264 73200	Markets for electrical products in Sweden Size and structure of current and future markets for: rotating machines, cables, transformers, switchgear and electrical accessories	£80

Source: Euan Blauvelt and Jennifer Durlacher (eds), *World Sources of Market Information*, vol 3, Gower Press, 1982. (Reproduced by kind permission of the publisher.)

Marketing in Small Businesses

With indirect exporting certain export houses, such as export merchants and confirming houses, will accept financing and credit risk but the supplying firm will have little or no control over the market. On the other hand, manufacturers' export agents will not usually accept the financial risk but also, would not normally handle competitors' products (Table 9.2).

With direct exporting the choices are much wider and include: international trading companies based in the host countries, commission agencies, overseas distributors and stockists and the establishment of branch offices abroad. The advantages and disadvantages of these forms of entry are contrasted in Table 9.3.

Some key problem areas

Most authors on international marketing point to the dangers of a basic export approach to establishing overseas trading. The basic reasons given relate to the pursuing of exports merely as a way of filling surplus capacity made vacant by a declining home market and that this approach is often haphazard in nature; the home firm merely grasping opportunities as they arise and with little sense of deliberation or direction.

In essence, planning for international marketing is governed much by the same principles as for home marketing, although the principles are much harder to put into practice. For example, identifying key markets ideally requires a global approach so that comparisons can be made and individual markets selected on the basis of their attractiveness. Secondly, entering overseas markets requires some expertise in searching out competent agents and thirdly, attention to marketing mix variables, in particular pricing and promotion, will almost certainly be required. In addition to these demands, the small business will be required to cope with complex documentation procedures, financial risks and a much greater sense of remoteness than experienced with the home market. It is not surprising then that unless the firm is blessed with a truly innovative product or other competitive advantages it may find the going difficult. Even if the firm felt it had something to offer, penetrating overseas markets effectively will require adherence to basic marketing principles.

Hy-Tran Engineering

Hy-Tran was facing a declining UK market in the early 1980s. They had recently developed a new product for a major customer and they hoped that this would provide an opportunity for increasing exports to European markets.

Table 9.2 Comparison of typical characteristics of UK export houses

Category of export house	Representation arrangement	Seeks	Accepts financing and credit risk (short-term)	Shipping insurance and documentation	Remuneration	Manufacturer's degree of control over market	Handles competing lines	Continuing relationship
Export merchant	Acts as principal	Customers abroad and suppliers in UK	Yes	Undertaken	Difference between purchase and resale prices	Nil	Yes	No
Confirming house	Confirms, as principal order placed by foreign buyer	Suppliers in UK	Yes	Undertaken	Commission from foreign buyer	Nil	Yes	No
Buying/indent house	Acts on behalf of foreign buyer either buying with wide discretion on orders received or placing indents on suppliers specified by buyer	Suppliers in UK	Yes if required	Undertaken	Commission from foreign buyer	Nil	Yes	No
Manufacturer's export agent	Represents UK manufacturers	Customers abroad	Not usually	Not normally undertaken	Commission from UK manufacturer	Fair	No	Yes
Specialist export manager	Represents UK manufacturers	Customers abroad	Sometimes	Undertaken	Commission from UK manufacturer plus retainer	Good	No	Yes

Source: L.S. Walsh, *International Marketing*, M&E Handbook, 1978, by permission of Pitman Publishing, London.

Table 9.3 Types of direct export entry points

Type of entry	Advantages	Disadvantages
Overseas agency	May agree to take credit risk; benefits of experience; low investment costs	Likely to carry competitors' products; require constant motivation; commission may be abnormally high
Distributors and/or stockist	Continuous exposure of product; willing to invest in stock, and spares, etc.	May command exclusive or preferential rights; no guarantee of marketing capability; will need constant motivation
Branch office	Closer market contact; dedicate sales effort; better chance of sustaining good customer service	Open to taxation by host government; capital investment required; continuing overhead burden

The company was particularly keen to penetrate the West German market, where they had a main agent, although little business had been generated over the past few years, in that country. Graham Jones, sales director, commented: 'I don't know whether it's the agent or just a condition of the market. The West Germans are probably quite advanced in this type of business and I expect they're more inclined to support their national industry, unless the product is revolutionary in some way. I think that what we have now will gain us a stronger foothold in the market.'

As the months went by Graham Jones began to realize that there was going to be very little change out of the German agent. (Hy-Tran hadn't had any serious enquiries for the new product, other than from a couple of UK companies.) Then, quite by accident, he came across a series of NEDO (National Economic Development Office) reports on the West German process plant industry (it had never been a regular activity of the company to gather overseas industry information, largely because few people had time to read such reports!). What he read gave him plenty of food for thought and he noted the following significant observations:

- West German companies would welcome direct contact with the manufacturer's representatives.
- An established sales office in West Germany would be a good idea.

- UK products were considered favourably, but ability to deliver on time was very questionable and this was based on real, past experiences.
- Ability to communicate in the host language was greatly respected.
- They appreciated a willingness by potential suppliers to advise on design and applications problems.

Graham Jones was the first to admit that he hadn't quite understood just what effort was needed to even get to the negotiation stage. Furthermore, he felt some guilt that he hadn't kept in regular contact with the West German agent or even knew much about the latter's ability to sell. He reflected: 'Exporting in this way seems like leaving things to chance. As long as you contact an agent you think everything will take off from there. It's obviously not as easy as that. Yet, I'm not sure we can do more than we are doing at present. For example, I don't think that we can run to the cost of a West German sales office nor can we afford to spend too much time chasing opportunities overseas.'

Conclusion

In these days of rationalization and cutbacks, these comments appear reasonable. However, in the absence of a positive commitment to overseas market development, it is hardly surprising that customer response should be unpredictable, at best. For example, supposing we, ourselves, were faced with a similar situation when considering purchase of a foreign-made product. It would probably need a first-class agent to make up for the type of exporter deficiencies suggested above and, of course, we might not even consider importing if home-based producers could meet our needs adequately. Ironically, Hy-Tran had recently installed some very sophisticated and expensive machines for computer-controlled cutting operations – imported from West Germany!

Capitalizing on opportunity

Identifying and stimulating overseas market opportunity is a marketing skill in itself, but taking such opportunity to its ultimate and successful conclusion will generally demand more in the way of sound preparation, good judgement and the acceptance that, however successful the firm is on its home ground, it must be prepared to modify its marketing approach to meet new conditions. Even when the

Marketing in Small Businesses

build-up to developing business may seem to be going to plan the obvious can be overlooked.

Automated Scanning Systems (ASS)

Following an international conference held in the Isle of Man, where the company had exhibited its systems, an approach was made by senior executives of an authority located some 10 miles south of Paris.

The French party made a visit to an installation in the north of England and were quite impressed with what they observed. Andy Sherratt, ASS's sales director, commented:

> 'I was very impressed with their command of English and as the discussions got down to the technicalities it was obvious they considered the system to be far superior to that of Prelac, our major competitor. Tim Purvis (head of the local authority department) seemed to do all the talking so we could never be accused of aggressive selling. While Prelac has the advantage of an international standing, our system is much more technologically advanced and we have the benefit of patent protection.'

Some weeks later Giles Carter, ASS's Southern Sales Manager and a qualified engineer, was sent to France to view the interested authority's manual system and to discuss the finer points of the proposed installation and operation. Coincidentally, he met Mike Fletcher, Prelac's sales manager, at Heathrow Airport, who was also flying to Paris. Giles and Mike had met in the Isle of Man and, as expected on such an important business occasion, they had taken advantage of the social scene.

Mike explained that he was combining business with pleasure but other than that, he wouldn't be drawn on specifics. The pair agreed to meet at a named Parisienne restaurant that evening and it was at this venue that Giles first experienced Mike's excellent command of the French language. Giles's own experience, however, proved to be less enlightening. Several days later he explained to Andy Sherratt:

> 'The day after I arrived I contacted Jacques Michelotti, head of the authority, and after lunch and a chat he introduced me to the library supervisor. From then on, I was stumped. The supervisor couldn't, or was reluctant to, speak English and my knowledge of French was limited to what I could recall from

Overseas marketing

'O' level studies. After about an hour I had this acute headache and I was beginning to doubt my own credibility. I must have had this mistaken idea that everybody I might come into contact with would speak English. I didn't even have product literature in the host language to fall back on, which would have at least saved me the trouble of describing the basic operation of the system. About an hour later I was introduced to a technician and I felt a bit more comfortable talking about the inner workings of the system although his English was no better than my French.'

Andy Sherratt seemed to take the conversation lightly,

'We didn't lose out to Prelac on your account. Nor is their product up to our standard. It's just that the company is big and has a name – it's as simple as that. Anyway, the powers-that-be knew how good our system was, so I don't think the supervisor would have influenced their decision in a contract of this value.'

Giles Carter felt some relief but deep down he couldn't agree with Andy Sherratt. He pondered on the fact that the French party had taken the trouble to visit the company and seen fit to invite him to France. He also recalled Mike Fletcher's command of the French language and his own disastrous presentation. 'You never get a second chance in this game,' he reflected.

Conclusion

The obvious is sometimes overlooked and although it may be no consolation to Giles Carter, he probably wasn't the first, nor would he be the last, to assume that language could ever be a problem in negotiating overseas business deals. This assumption is often seen by many professional observers as pure arrogance, but, more than anything, it is probably simple ignorance of the implications. Supposing the tables had been turned and the company had felt obliged to visit a French supplier in order to negotiate a purchase. How might they have reacted had their hosts insisted on conducting the negotiations in the French language? Similarly, the assumption that the library supervisor would have little or no say in the decision-making process was probably very far from the truth. Even if this assumption was based on experiences in the UK market, it is folly to assume that overseas customers will automatically behave in a similar manner.

Marketing in Small Businesses

Problems of managing documentation[1]

Exporting is often regarded as being more complex than domestic trade. Products may have to be modified and, apart from the language and tariff barriers, dealing with documentation is an extra, daunting task for the small firm. Not only is the range of documents required substantial, such as order processing, invoicing, insurance, customs declaration, shipping instructions, transport documents, etc., but some countries may require as many as six to eight copies of the invoice and some may demand that such information be in their own language.

The cost of errors can be disruptive, to say the least.

Pantronic Limited

Pantronic attended an international exhibition in Holland during 1976. At the end of the exhibition, salesman Paul Shrimpling loaded the exhibits in his estate car with the intention of driving down to Munich. There he was to demonstrate the company's range of electronic sensors to a potential customer who could not be present at the exhibition. This visit had been arranged well before the actual dates of the exhibition were known and, having a few days to spare, Paul spent some time touring Amsterdam and the surrounding area.

When he eventually arrived at the Dutch/German border he handed over the appropriate documentation to the customs along with his passport. Some minutes elapsed while the customs official went over the documents and he suddenly began to speak hurriedly – in Dutch – while pointing to one of the many documents.

This went on for several more minutes but Paul was none the wiser. Eventually, a Dutch lorry driver came out of what was now a lengthy queue and, after a few words with the official, he explained to Paul: 'Your documents are invalid. The dates shown indicate that the named equipment should have been back in the UK three days ago.'

Paul then remembered that the documentation had been prepared for the duration of the exhibition after the arrangements with the German company had been made. He had notified the sales department of the trip to Munich and had automatically assumed the documents would cover for the latter. He remarked to the lorry driver: 'Is there anything I can do to get the equipment to Germany? It's very important business and all my return arrangements have been made.'

After a short discussion with the official, the lorry driver explained: 'You must re-type all of the documentation with the correct dates. There is an office about 50 yards up the road and there, the clerk will assist you. Once this is done you must return here.'

About an hour later, Paul returned to the customs office where now the queue had grown considerably. By the time he got through customs and recovered his passport, he noticed that the delay had cost him over three hours in precious time.

On his return to the UK by ferry, some days later, he met up with two publishers' representatives who were returning from a book fair. Having recounted his misfortune, the representatives also explained that they had gone through a similar situation. They had listed the goods on their documentation as '50 children's books'. The customs official had asked: 'Were they all the same?' to which the reply was negative. 'Then,' said the official, 'You will have to type out every individual title.'

The conversation produced a few laughs, and it was agreed that the customs officials concerned had been completely unreasonable and that the UK customs would never be that inflexible in applying the rules.

On his way through the Nothing-to-Declare section, Paul was stopped by Customs and a search revealed an extra bottle of spirits over and above the allowance, which had 'slipped his mind'. As he drove away, minus the bottle and with a caution ringing in his ears, he had modified his original views somewhat. To be told that he had been 'let off lightly' was hard to swallow.

Conclusion

Accurate and comprehensive documentation is vital and, where necessary, it pays to check all angles. Paul might well have had one or two hard words in mind for the sales department, but as he was going to be at the sharp-end of the operation, it was in his best interest to make doubly sure. This is even more important where language and cultural barriers may hamper the proceedings and where the documentation represents the only effective mode of information communication.

Obtaining practical help and advice

For any small business contemplating exporting, or improving existing overseas business, possibly the most comprehensive source of help and advice is the British Overseas Trade Board (BOTB). Operating through ten regional (or acting regional) offices in the UK, the BOTB provides support to industry ranging from free overseas market information to financial assistance towards participation in overseas

Marketing in Small Businesses

trade fairs. The following represents a summary of some of the services available from the BOTB.[2] (See Appendix for regional offices' locations.)

Product data store

As part of its market information service, the BOTB has established a computerized microfilm database of product- and industry-based information on overseas markets. This includes information on market size and structure and market shares with particular reference to Britain's top export markets.

Export Intelligence Service (EIS)

EIS deals with general market information and export opportunities from around the world sent by nearly two hundred British Overseas Diplomatic posts. EIS covers overseas enquiries for products or services, agents seeking UK principals, early notification of projects overseas and other items offering new trade opportunities. Computer matching ensures that the client firm is sent only selected information appropriate to its needs. A nominal fee is payable, although some information is provided free of charge.

Export marketing research scheme

The board offers free professional advice on how to set about a research project and in many cases, offers generous grants towards the cost of the research.

Export representative service

The board provides information on potential overseas representatives which best match the profile of the client firm. For example, the commercial operations and standing of the businessmen, the extent of territory they cover and the back-up facilities they offer. The cost of the service varies according to the overseas country or countries involved.

Overseas status report service

This service provides:

- Trading interests and capabilities of a specified foreign company made known to the firm through introduction or direct approach.
- The scope of its activities.

Overseas marketing

- Any other agencies including British, already held.
- What territory it can effectively cover as agent or distributor.
- Its warehousing and distribution facilities and sales force.
- Its technical know-how and its after-sales servicing facilities.

The charge for the service as at 1987 was £24.15 including VAT.

Trade fairs overseas

Through its Fairs and Promotions Branch the BOTB provides help to groups of British exporters exhibiting at overseas trade fairs which in the view of BOTB appear to be sufficiently worthwhile. Assistance is usually in the form of individual exhibition stands with appropriate display aids, stands are provided at attractive rates, particularly to first-time exhibitors.

Technical help to exporters

This service has been developed due to the need for compliance with a variety of standards, laws and regulations demanded by potential target countries. Where product certification or approval schemes exist, matching such needs becomes a marketing necessity. Fees vary according to the amount of searching involved although if the information is at hand, it may cost nothing. First-time users (less than 200 employees) qualify for generous discounts.

With the emphasis on developing industry and community links, many colleges, polytechnics and universities are now geared to helping small firms tackle a wide variety of business problems. In some cases, academic staff may be seconded to industry for a short period as part of an officially authorized programme and work on problem-oriented tasks is encouraged. Other than out-of-pocket expenses, the service is generally free of charge to the employing firm. Library facilities and on-line data bases in many institutions provide an opportunity for the small firm to carry out exploratory market and industry research and there is always a chance that a particular investigation could form the basis for, say, an undergraduate or student group project. There is nothing lost in exploring such low-cost alternatives and often much to be gained.

Contractual arrangements

Once an opportunity arises for entering an overseas market, much thought will need to be given to establishing the terms of agreement with regard to distribution and/or other rights. The following extract

Marketing in Small Businesses

serves to illustrate the finer points of an actual draft agreement drawn up between a UK supplier, Bema Ltd, and an American distributor, Kalma Co. (names and products have been disguised).

Exclusive distributorship agreement

Bema has agreed to make Kalma the exclusive distributor of its patented clamping devices (products) in North America (the territory) for up to three (3) years.

Kalma hereby accepts such appointment and agrees diligently to solicit sales of products in the territory. Bema agree to assign to Kalma any orders that Bema receive for products to be delivered in the territory.

Kalma agrees by no later than 28 February 1987 to purchase and maintain an inventory of product with an aggregate cost of sixty thousand dollars ($60,000). By August 1988 such minimum inventory will have a cost of one hundred and thirty thousand dollars ($130,000).

Bema shall immediately give Kalma all its information concerning markets in the territory for the products including all files concerning Bema's prospective customers. Bema shall turn over to Kalma all advertising and promotional material and displays that Bema has available for use in the territory. Bema agrees at its expense to arrange at mutually agreeable times for appropriate key personnel to travel to the territory to assist Kalma with its marketing. Bema agrees promptly to process and ship Kalma's orders for the products.

Bema agrees that it shall be solely responsible for any commission, sale agency fee, or other similar charge payable in connection with direct sales of the products by Bema to customers in the territory.

Resale pricing of the products shall be at the sole discretion of Kalma.

Bema shall identify and defend Kalma and hold Kalma harmless against all liability, cost, and expense (including reasonable attorney's fees) resulting from any claims, demands, judgements and actions arising out of any property damage or injury, by whomever suffered, caused by manufacturing defect or failure of the products.

This extract is only a very small part of the total agreement document, but it is clear that expert advice will need to be sought with regard to the subsequent wording of agreements and the implications therein. As it happened in the above case, both parties made substantial alterations to the original document before reaching mutual agreement. Furthermore, they subsequently entered into a manufacturing licence agreement which involved more soul searching and the inevitable paperwork:

Manufacturing licence agreement (draft)

Kalma desire to obtain Bema's (licensor's) technology with respect to the manufacture of the products, licensor hereby grants Kalma's exclusive use in the territory, a licence under the patents listed in schedule 1 hereto to manufacture the products during the term of this agreement. This agreement in no way limits Kalma's right to export the products outside of the territory provided, however, that this agreement does not purport to grant Kalma a licence under licensor's patents issued under the laws of any jurisdiction besides the territory. Licensor further agrees:

- to furnish Kalma with complete product drawings and production information necessary for commercial manufacture of the products;
- to furnish Kalma with design engineering information, technical data, manufacturing drawings and instruction in methods of commercial manufacture of the products; and
- to assist Kalma generally, at Kalma's request in all phases of its manufacturing procedures for the products.

In consideration for all technological benefits afforded to Kalma under this agreement, Kalma agrees to pay licensor a lump sum fee of United States dollars eighty-five thousand ($85,000) and to pay to licensor, within sixty (60) days after the end of each quarter, a licence fee of two and one-half per cent (2.5%) of Kalma's net sales of the products during such quarter. 'Net sales', for the purpose of this agreement shall mean the gross sales price of the products sold by Kalma, less only commercial, trade or cash discounts and adjustments actually allowed by Kalma. Kalma shall, at no further cost to Kalma, have the right to use Bema's trademarks for the products.

This agreement shall continue in effect for a period of ten (10) years from the effective date, subject to early termination as provided herein. Ten (10) years from the effective date, subject to earlier termination of this agreement as provided herein, Kalma shall have the paid-up, perpetual, non-exclusive right to use the technology that shall have been transferred to Kalma through such latter date. Kalma may terminate this agreement upon sixty (60) days' notice to Bema. Upon termination of this agreement

Marketing in Small Businesses

for whatever cause, Kalma agrees not to use the licensed technology to manufacture or sell the products for a period ending ten (10) years from the effective date.

It is probably understandable that an overseas agency will try to get the best possible deal and cover for liability; particularly where the host country's laws are extremely exacting and very often put into practice. Needless to say, the exporting firm should also negotiate for a fair and reasonable exchange and be prepared to question and think through what appear to be undue clauses.

Case study: Woods of Windsor[3]

Fortune smiled on Roger Knowles when he made the decision to move from Keighley, Yorkshire, where he had been running a successful retail pharmacy, to the Woods Pharmacy in the historic town of Windsor. The 200-year-old pharmacy had been sadly neglected and Roger and his wife Kathleen were faced with a daunting task by the condition of the premises and the run-down state of the business. The Knowles family moved in – quite literally 'over the shop' – and started

Photo copyright: Woods of Windsor Ltd, Windsor, Berkshire, 1988.

on the mammoth chore of clearing out the accumulation of two centuries. The assorted rubbish that crammed the five-storey building from cellar to attic was, however, to reveal a priceless treasure trove.

Having cleared the cellar and lower floors the Knowles braced themselves to ferry yet more debris from the third storey rooms, and it was here that Roger made his discovery: around eighty ancient recipe and prescription books, some dating back to the turn of the last century, had been abandoned to dust, rust and mould, but the majority – even those written in faded copperplate handwriting – were still legible. Their fascination was immediate to a qualified pharmacist like Roger Knowles, whose interest in the historical aspects of his profession fortuitously saved a remarkable and unique pharmaceutical archive from joining the rest of the discarded rubbish.

The prescription books, which painstakingly record the ailments and treatment of, among others, visiting royalty and local dignitaries, bear witness to the standing and pedigree of the Woods Pharmacy in the late nineteenth century. But it was the formularies, with their traditional recipes for pot pourri, toilet waters and the like, that suggested to the new owners the possibility of developing a collection of perfumed products that could be sold in the small room at the rear of the existing chemist shop.

At that time, says Roger Knowles, he had no thought of being anything other than a pharmacist, but the introduction of an 'own brand' range of fragranced gifts based on the traditional recipes not only seemed a logical extension of the business, but offered a potentially lucrative sideline in a town that annually attracts thousands of visitors from all over the globe. The Knowles felt that the fragranced products they envisaged would have particular appeal to visitors, being attractive, useful, easily portable, not to mention the fact that they would be linked historically to the source. An unbeatable combination.

And so it proved to be pot pourri (spelt with one 'r' in the original recipe) that was the first recipe to be tried and the couple put the fragrant results of their blendings into pretty lace sachets – charming, inexpensive items that remain an important and popular feature of the Woods of Windsor collection some fifteen years later. Kathleen Knowles can still ruefully recall making up lavender and pot pourri sachets by candlelight during the power-cuts and 'three-day weeks' of the early 1970s.

It soon became evident that the concept of attractively presented, traditionally formulated fragrant gifts was acceptable not only to the residents and visitors to Windsor but to a much wider market. When the range had developed to the point where it included some twenty different items, Roger Knowles set forth with a case of samples to try

Marketing in Small Businesses

his luck with some of the major London department stores. The Woods of Windsor collection was enthusiastically received and the pressure was on to develop and extend the scope of the range, to introduce new products, and to create an attractive and harmonious packaging programme.

By 1974 a small warehouse in Windsor had become available and Roger Knowles decided to relinquish his connection with the pharmacy business and devote himself full time to the task of being a manufacturer and supplier of fragrant gifts. 'And then,' he says, 'the work really began.'

Today, in addition to the original retail premises – much enlarged and refurbished, with the upper floors given over to office and administrative accommodation – this thriving company has warehouse, manufacturing and distribution premises at nearby Colnbrook and, since February this year, further accommodation at Poyle where such items as the new custom-made gift baskets are assembled.

From twenty products in 1974 to over two hundred items in 1985: spectacular progress that more than justified the Knowles' decision to enter the hazardous area of manufacture and supply. Quality – both in the product itself and in its presentation – is one of the keys to success of the Woods of Windsor range which can be divided under two main headings: personal toiletries and fragrances for the home.

The Toiletries Collection (in eight subtle flower fragrances) embraces everything from fine soaps, talcum powder, bath cubes and bath and shower gels, to eau de toilette, concentrated perfume, shampoo, hand and body lotion plus a variety of charming gift sets, travel sets and lovely custom-made baskets filled with assorted toiletry items, these last being the most recent addition to the collection. There is also, of course, the phenomenally successful Woods of Windsor for Gentlemen range in its restrained masculine packaging adorned with the Windsor Castle motif taken from an old engraving circa 1820.

The soaps, which are all tissue-wrapped and individually boxed with three of a kind contained in an outer box to enable the retailer to sell them individually as well as in boxes of three, typify the thought and standards of quality that have gone into the production of the entire collection. Triple milled to produce a long-lasting, high-quality hard soap that will not crack, the 100g tablets are produced with a gently rounded contour to make them feel as good as they look and smell. Lanolin is added to give a rich, creamy lather but, apart from a small amount of caramel in the gentlemen's range, no colouring dyes are used. Regardless of the individual perfume, every tablet of soap is white: to match any bathroom suite and to reduce the dangers of skin reaction which can occur when dyes are present.

The toilet waters are supplied in pump atomizers and not aerosols, these being unacceptable on grounds of ecology, as fluorocarbon aerosols are considered harmful to the environment. Aerosols are only used for men's deodorant and shaving foam – and these contain a non-harmful hydrocarbon propellant.

In January 1983 the company introduced Travel Miniatures, delightful and practical sets comprising 25g soap, soap traveller, 30g talc, 30 ml bath gel, shampoo, and hand/body lotion, all contained in a plastic drawstring sac. This year Woods of Windsor have brought out yet another lovely accessory for the traveller, the Travel Companion – a cleverly designed fabric toilet bag (complete with hanging ring) which opens out flat to give access to the contents – a repeat of that of the Travel Miniature with the addition of a face cloth.

Travel Miniature, Travel Companion and Travel Wallet feature in the Woods of Windsor for Gentlemen range. This robust and very popular series was inspired by a formula in one of the old books. Called Spanish Leather or Peau d'Espagna, it was originally created to perfume leather products which smelt unpleasant after the tanning process. It is a vigorous yet subtly spicy fragrance that has proved enormously successful. The range covers a total of twenty-nine products, including gift sets and accessories such as shaving brush and shaving mug with soap.

The Fragrance for the Home collection is headed, naturally enough, by the Nottingham lace drawer sachets which were the first Woods of Windsor fragranced gifts. In the early days Kathleen Knowles purchased her lace from a nearby Windsor store; today the company uses something like 700 miles of lace to produce a series of variously fragranced sachets in assorted sizes and styles – all beautifully packaged in the company's house style. Pot pourri too still features in the range – in gift boxes, baskets, sachets and in loose sacks to enable stockists to sell it by the scoopful. Refresher oils are also offered.

Of all the products produced by Woods of Windsor, the Perfumed Drawer Liners, the first to appear on the UK market, have been by far the most successful. The delicious designs of Honeysuckle, Lavender, Lily of the Valley and Rose featured on the liner papers are the basis of this supplement and are repeated in miniaturized form on some of the latest packaging. In 1979 the company won a design award for their fragranced drawer-lining papers which come handsomely boxed, with six sheets to a box, the design of which matches the contents.

In addition, Woods of Windsor offer a series of Room Fragrance sprays – lavender, rose, traditional pot pourri, and cinnamon and orange pot pourri – plus an ingenious Vapourizing Room Fragrance. This latter uses a metal vapourizing ring which is placed on top of a

Marketing in Small Businesses

table lamp bulb, a few drops of the scented oil being poured into the ring which gives off a subtle fragrance as the oil is vapourized by the heat of the bulb.

Woods of Windsor products are known throughout the world: the company export to more than forty countries and have, since 1980, an established subsidiary, Woods of Windsor (USA), in Garden City, Long Island, New York, to handle sales and distribution of the British-made products throughout the United States. The USA is by far the largest of the Windsor company's export markets, but Japan too accounts for a major slice of overseas sales.

Some facts

By mid 1987 Woods of Windsor's turnover had grown to £4.5 million, with sale increases in the past doubling each year, when growth settled at a 50 per cent annual rise. Due to the decline in the Australian dollar, sales in that country had been badly hit and the company had considered starting up its own operation to reduce the distribution margins. In general, currency changes had taken a toll of exports. However, the company was doing extremely well in Japan selling through some three hundred department stores – pot-pourri incidentally, being made up by local manufacturers.

In 1981 when Roger Knowles decided to enter the Japanese market, he had to face bureaucratic needs such as registering perfumery formulas and shipments analyses. In 1986 the company introduced the designer fragrance range, 'Rondaletia'. This had taken three years and a cost of £100,000 to launch.

The company first ventured into export in 1975 when Roger Knowles, equipped once again with sample cases, spent two weeks in the USA cold calling on stores and retail outlets. In 1983 Woods of Windsor gained a Queens Award for Export and today export sales account for some 45 per cent of the company's turnover. Also growing is the hotel market which has, Roger Knowles believes, enormous potential.

Design has always been an important aspect of the British company's presentation. 'Attractive packaging gives the customer the instinct to buy,' says Roger Knowles. From labels, to containers and boxes, the Woods of Windsor 'look' – created by their own specially commissioned designer – is harmonious, fresh and appealing. Product planning and presentation is a continuous evolutionary process, with new product launches being scheduled on a twice-yearly basis.

The company operates a policy of 'selective distribution', and Woods of Windsor products are to be found in department stores, good gift shops and some speciality shops all over the world. Point-of-sale units can be supplied, provided that the required stock order is sufficient, and there are also a number of other sales aids available such as shelf strips, showcards, and special displays. Visual presentation of the product is all important: as can be seen from Woods of Windsor's own delightful retail shop on the ground floor of the premises in Windsor where the original concept was born in a 200-year-old chemist shop.

Points for deliberation

- What is Woods' product concept?
- What element of the Woods' overseas marketing strategy appears to have contributed to their success in Japan?
- Which particular environment factors are sensitive in the Japanese market and why?
- What key environmental factor appears sensitive to all of the export markets covered?
- What is Woods' distinctive competence and in what way can this be used to build up further growth, particularly in exports?
- What strategy might be necessary to revive the Australian market?
- What aspect of the product line is likely to appeal to the American market?
- Given the 'environmental' variations in the different export markets covered, what elements of the marketing mix (if any), would require modification?

Case study: Almo-Cut[4]

When inventor Paul Adcock took his plastic mower blades to Cologne's Garden Trade Fair, he hoped he'd sell enough to cover the cost of his stand. Now he's still reeling from the shock of £16 million worth of orders which sets his family company firmly on the map – and promises to make him a millionaire.

His Almo-Cut SupaSafe, claimed to be the world's first completely safe blade for rotary mowers, landed orders from the USA, Canada, Australia, Sweden, Holland, Germany, and several other countries. To cope with it all, his workforce of eight at Alwoodley Lawnmowers in Chapel Allerton, Leeds, is soon to be expanded to 14 and within eighteen months to 50, and the company will be looking for larger premises. Banks who just a few months ago had told him to 'get his act together' before they would consider investment are now suddenly very eager to talk business. 'It's unbelievable,' said Mr Adcock. 'People kept saying "who the hell are they?" – now they know. It was quite amazing the amount of attention we attracted.'

Marketing in Small Businesses

Photo copyright: Almo-Cut, Leeds, 1988.

   Throughout the three-day show a video was running on the Almo-Cut stand demonstrating just how revolutionary the blade is. It showed Paul Adcock thrusting his foot into the swirling cutters with no damage. It was the plight of a friend who had lost part of his foot in a mower accident that five years ago sent Mr Adcock into his garden workshed with a passionate determination to design a safe, non-metal blade. He worked away through years of frustration, a £90,000 investment and second mortgage to finally emerge with a compound plastic granule solution which, when hard, is almost unbreakable. The blades, retail price £4.95, can be sharpened with a file and Almo-Cut give an unconditional guarantee of satisfaction. Each blade is expected to have a lifetime of about 18 to 24 months, according to use.
   Before Cologne, Mr Adcock said that British interest in his product had been 'pathetic to say the least'. His company had sent out information about the range of blades to major mower manufacturers and only one company, ALKO of Britain, had bothered to reply. ALKO now offer a choice of standard or safety blades on all their 12-inch electric mowers.

Overseas marketing

The instant success that Cologne has brought Paul Adcock makes little difference to his long-term objectives. His biggest priority is to improve safety research facilities. He is already working on a SupaSafe blade for hedge-cutters. He is very flattered that a German company has asked him to help in an R&D project with which they have a problem. Another company, Armatron, from the USA, is keen to adapt his SupaSafe blade for fitting into their garden shredder. And although Mr Adcock is adamant he wants to stay in Britain, there have been approaches from abroad for him to set up production there.

Points for deliberation

- What is the unique selling proposition (USP) of Paul Adcock's product?
- Which element of the marketing mix appears to have contributed significantly to the success of the launch?
- What potential threats face the future business?
- In planning for the future, what changes in the current overseas marketing strategy might be anticipated?

Notes

1 At the time of writing, UK export documentation was the subject of major redesign and rationalization.
2 Extracted from 'Help for exporters', *British Overseas Trade Board*, 1986–7.
3 Cotter, V. (1985) *Gifts International*, September (reproduced by kind permission of Benn Publications Ltd, Tonbridge).
4 Blackford, J. (1987) 'Thanks a million', *Garden Trade News*, November, 1–2.

Further Reading

Gilligan, C. and Hird, M. (1986) *International Marketing*, London: Croom Helm.
Davis, G. (1984) *Managing Export Distribution*, London: Heinemann.
Noonan, C. (1985) *Practical Export Management*, George Allen and Unwin.

10 Marketing to MOD

Synopsis

For the smaller enterprise, attempting to do business with government departments can be fraught with difficulties. Often it is a case of not knowing whom to approach or trying to meet exacting and unfamiliar quality-control standards, in addition to coping with a jungle of paperwork. Even where a company has the necessary capabilities to compete for contracts, the actual cost of bidding for business can, in itself, be prohibitive.

In recent years some of these problems have gradually been reduced by new government measures. For example, the MOD Small Firms Initiative which was set up in 1986, has sought out small companies, through chambers of commerce and enterprise agencies, in an attempt to encourage more contact and active involvement in defence business. In 1986 to 1987 small companies accounted for 13 per cent of UK defence equipment expenditure and a much larger share was taken by this sector via sub-contracting work for the larger (prime) contractors.

Problems of marketing

In some respects, the identification of customer needs is less of a problem than in many commercial markets. In most cases, the customer (government department) will spell out the requirements in the form of an invitation-to-tender and this will include the performance specification of the product or service in question, the quality requirements, delivery schedule and any contractual obligations.

Aside from the problems of ensuring it is constantly aware of contract opportunities and maintaining the capability to respond, the smaller enterprise has to understand the implications of actually securing the business. For example, the degree to which the customer specification is defined and how this may affect predictions of research and development progress, delivery, and the likely cost of subsequent default. On a more general level, the smaller enterprise may have difficulties in trying to serve both government and its commercial markets simultaneously. The differences in behaviour between the two sectors has implications for the firm's internal organization such as accounting, production, and quality-assurance systems, while the differences in environmental factors may enforce the adoption of entirely different strategies. There is an obvious cost in serving radically different market segments as can be seen in the larger organizations, where divisionalization is deemed necessary.

In spite of the attractiveness of the government market – for example, defence equipment expenditure was some £86 million in 1987 – there is really only one customer being courted by many suppliers and thus, bargaining power is largely one-sided. In many cases, volume-production opportunity is limited, communication bottlenecks can occur and the firm needs to be persistent and patient in dealing with the inevitable bureaucracy.

However, as pointed out in the introduction, market entry is being supported and encouraged, and in the following sections the procedures for initiating contact and pursuing defence business, is outlined in some detail.

Background[1]

The Ministry of Defence is a large, complex and security-conscious organization, for the very good, if obvious, reason that, under the political direction of its Secretary of State, it is responsible for the security of the nation, and for the vast management task which that entails. Many small firms feel that it is not worth trying to break into such a monolith, or that their goods and services will be too mundane for defence needs. The aim of this chapter is to overcome such misconception.

MOD is the largest single customer of British industry, and in some sectors it is the dominant customer. In recent years defence procurement has accounted for, for example, about half the output of the aerospace industry and one-third of the output of the electronics and shipbuilding industries. Further, in many sectors (e.g. electronics, aviation control systems, and marine technology) the Ministry provides – through its own research and development establishments and extramural research and development contracts – much of the R and D support without which those industrial sectors could not function effectively.

In all, more than 90 per cent of defence equipment expenditure is

Marketing in Small Businesses

spent in the UK, supporting no fewer than 242,000 jobs directly in British industry and another 193,000 indirectly. MOD procurement of non-equipment items supports a total of 160,000 jobs and sales of defence equipment abroad another 145,000. At any one time more than 10,000 British companies are working on defence contracts, and the Ministry may place as many as 30,000 contracts a year through its headquarters purchasing organization alone.

The nature of defence business does mean that a certain proportion of MOD contracts are specialized. In the defence equipment programme in particular, certain major projects require the use of advanced technology, involve special development programmes, and can only be put into production by certain suppliers. But small firms have a part to play in this process; and it is open to any firm to apply for – and, if competitive, to succeed in obtaining – defence business.

MOD organization and contact points

It is always important for a firm seeking new business to find out as much as possible about the potential customer and his needs. For a small firm hoping to sell to the Ministry, this basic information can be difficult to obtain.

There are a network of contact points within the purchasing areas of MOD to whom firms can turn for advice and information. It is important to understand how these contact points fit into the organization of the Ministry as a whole (see Fig. 10.1).

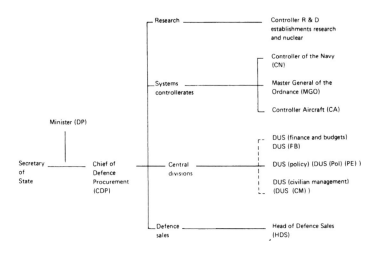

Figure 10.1 MOD/PE organisation (1987)

Basic MOD organization

The MOD consists of five elements under the political direction of the Secretary of State for Defence. These are:

- *The central staffs* responsible for defence policy and planning as a whole.
- *The three Service Departments* (the Navy, Army and Air Force departments) responsible for management of each of the three services in terms of operational requirements, organization, training, personnel and logistics.
- *The Procurement Executive (PE)* responsible for the central procurement both of equipment for all three Services from research through to production, and of other goods and services. The PE maintains a close working relationship with the Service Departments and with industry, and also helps industry to sell defence equipment abroad.

The PE is headed by the Chief of Defence Procurement (CDP) under the political direction of Ministers, and comprises:

1 The central divisions under the Deputy Under-Secretary (Policy) (PE) are responsible for procurement policy (including industrial and international aspects, purchasing and contracts policy, and quality-assurance arrangements).
2 The three Systems Controllerates are headed by:
Controller of the Navy (C of N) responsible for the procurement of Sea Systems equipment for the three Services;
Master General of the Ordnance (MGO) responsible for the procurement of land systems equipment for the three Services; and
Controller Aircraft (CA) responsible for the procurement of air systems equipment for the three Services. (For example, CA procures helicopters for all three Services.)

The Systems Controllers' staffs of civilian and Service officers maintain close liaison with the Service staffs responsible for such matters as operational requirements and logistics. Below Controller level the Systems Controllerates are arranged into general equipment groupings at Director-General level, within which responsibility for groups of related projects is allocated to project directors and project managers. Financial and contractual matters are grouped in each Controllerate under an Assistant Under-Secretary and a Principal Director of Contracts respectively. Only contracts staff (or designated local purchase officers) have the power to commit the Ministry contractually.

3   The Controllerate R and D establishments, Research and Nuclear headed by Controller R and D Establishments Research and Nuclear (CERN), responsible for the R and D establishments and for the research programme carried out in the establishments and also by contract extramurally. The establishments also provide support to Systems Controllerates' project managers, by giving advice on the technical oversight of projects and by providing test and trials facilities.

4   The Defence Sale Organization (DSO) promotes the sale of UK-manufactured defence equipment to other countries and gives advice and assistance to industry. Advice on specific markets is provided by four regional marketing directors each responsible for a group of countries. More general information on worldwide equipment markets is given by the Director of Marketing Services who also acts as the initial contact point for firms new to the DSO.

Market entry

The three entry methods, in order of likely interest to small firms are through:

- Sub-contract opportunities
- Local purchase orders
- Direct contract opportunities

In a special category of direct contract opportunities are those requirements covered by the EC Supplies Directive and by the GATT Agreement on Government Procurement (See Annex 1 p.188).

Sub-contract opportunities

Probably the best chance for a small firm to obtain defence business is as a sub-contractor from one of the major defence contractors – or indeed from other defence subcontractors themselves.

In a drive to reduce costs and staff numbers and in the interests of efficient project management, the Ministry of Defence are seeking to place more and more defence contracts in the hands of a single prime contractor. Such defence contracts, in their turn, almost invariably involve a number of sub-system contractors and component suppliers. In such cases, the Ministry's role in the day-to-day management of the contract is a limited one; the general rule is that it is for the prime contractor to choose his own sub-contractors. Thus it is to the defence prime contractors that small firms need to address themselves.

The MOD does not believe they should intervene in the relationship between prime and sub-contractors; but just as they recognize that their purchasing power should be used to enhance industrial performance, so they hope that defence contractors will use their purchasing power in a similar way within the national economy. But it is also up to small firms themselves to win orders from prime contractors by convincing them of the quality of the goods and services they have to offer. It is not necessary for a firm to be registered with the MOD contracts administration branch for it to undertake sub-contract work on MOD orders, although a prime contractor will want to assure himself of the firm's quality standards.

The MOD does not assess firms who operate only as sub-contractors in defence work. However, MOD have recognized a new independent scheme of assessed capability established and operated under the auspices of the British Standards Institution and based on British Standard 5750. The selection for defence sub-contract work of a firm registered by BSI under this scheme will be regarded by MOD assessment teams and quality-assurance representatives as equivalent to the use of an MOD-assessed and registered firm.

Local purchases

Most major defence establishments have delegated purchasing powers. At some, particularly the R & D establishments, these powers are quite high and involve large numbers of contracts; but even local service units generally have day-to-day requirements which it is most cost-effective to meet locally. There are many such establishments up and down the country. Invitations to tender are issued from the establishment itself and the point of entry is through the local purchase officer.

Generally, purchases under these arrangements require less extensive assessment procedures than are necessary before a direct headquarters contract can be placed, and local purchase officers consequently have access to a wider field of suppliers.

Direct contract opportunities

Direct contracts are those awarded by a headquarters contract branch of the Ministry; they cover not only the main defence equipment projects, but also all the principal defence contracts which are handled centrally, including, for example, those for maintenance and spares. Many such contracts do, of course, go to major defence contractors but a significant number are awarded each year to smaller firms, once they have satisfied the Ministry both as to their commercial viability and their technical competence.

Contracts branch administration

Whatever type of goods or services firms wish to offer the MOD, they are required to contact, in the first instance, contracts branch administration. This contracts branch maintains a register of all potential suppliers and act as a clearing house through which firms can make their products or services known to project staff in the various purchasing areas of the MOD (see Annex 2).

A firm is required to write or telephone, giving brief but concrete details of the goods and services it offers, and mentioning any capacity it might have for research and development work. This information is then circulated to interested procurement branches. If MOD see advantage in including the firm as a potential direct supplier, they will send a confidential questionnaire for the firm to complete, asking for details of financial position, names of referees including bankers, details of facilities available, management and other staff (e.g. the number and trades of employees), and the extent and capacity of the plant. If the check on the commercial viability of the firm is satisfactory, normally MOD will then arrange for an assessment team to visit the firm to assess its technical competence (see 'Quality assurance' below).

Principles and types of contract

Because MOD are responsible for obtaining value for public money, they are concerned with the financial, organizational, and technical reliability of contractors as well as with the competitiveness of their pricing.

In selecting the number of firms to be invited to tender for a particular contract, MOD take into account the size of the order, firms' technical expertise and capacity and any previous record in the relevant field. Those invited will usually include any firms holding design rights in the equipment concerned, the strong contenders amongst past tenderers or suppliers, any UK priority suppliers, e.g. those employing the blind and disabled, and firms in designated development areas. The general aim is to keep the field of potential contractors as broad as possible and to observe the principles of competition to the greatest possible extent during the various stages of procurement. Thus wherever possible MOD invite tenders from a number of potential suppliers.

However, because of the specialized nature of MOD requirements, a high proportion of contracts for design, development and initial production of major items of defence equipment are necessarily placed with selected firms without competition. Such non-competitive contracts are also placed when only one firm has the relevant capacity or technical experience to do the work, or in cases of extreme urgency, or when a firm has proprietary rights in a design.

Contracts placed with small firms following competition will normally be at fixed prices determined by the competition. Non-competitive contracts are however priced in one of two ways. Either (1) a fixed price or, comparatively rarely, a target price, is agreed on the basis of estimates of costs formulated before or during the performance of the work, or (2) the price is established on the basis of actual costs ascertained after work is finished. A fixed price or other incentive arrangement is preferred to a cost-plus percentage profit contract, but will normally be possible only where a well-defined specification and a well-founded cost estimate exist. The profit element included is based on a formula, with differential rates for non-risk and risk work, agreed periodically between the government and the Confederation of British Industry. Certain higher-value fixed-price contracts include provision for the Ministry to carry out selective post-costing investigation as a check on estimating techniques, to help in the pricing of follow-on contracts and to scrutinize the outcome. An independent Review Board for Government Contracts exists to adjudicate on individual contracts referred to it when one of the parties considers an excessive profit or unconscionable loss has been made. These arrangements are unlikely to apply to lower-value contracts.

Contract conditions

It is important that firms seeking MOD business understand the conditions on which contracts are based.

MOD make extensive use of special conditions which are incorporated where necessary by reference into tender and contract documents. Most of these conditions belong to a series of documents called DEFCONS. These will be called up in the contract which will also indicate where firms can obtain them.

Contract financing

The MOD as a purchaser does not undertake the funding of contractors' requirements for capital, although interim payments may be available in contracts of long duration or when investment in work in progress is heavy. In the case of contracts awarded following competition, interim payments will normally not be made unless agreed at the outset as a condition of the contract.

Marketing in Small Businesses

Quality assurance

MOD normally place contracts only with firms whose arrangements for quality and product reliability give the confidence to reduce their own direct inspection to a minimum level or even to dispense with it entirely. It is policy to restrict direct contract opportunities as far as practicable to firms with satisfactory quality-assurance arrangements. Should a direct contractor choose to sub-contract work, he remains responsible for its quality: BS5750, referred to in Section 1 on sub-contract opportunities, is also relevant here.

Confidence in a direct contractor's quality-control arrangements is based on assessment for compliance with one of the various quality assurance Defence Standards which stipulate requirements for levels of quality control and inspection organizations appropriate to the contract technical requirements.

These Defence Standards do not refer to products and thus apply over the whole procurement field. They concern themselves solely with specifying those elements for a quality management system which the contractor must have if MOD is to be assured that it will receive products of the required quality. Tender and contract documents always state the Defence Standard required.

Annex 1: EC and GATT

Items covered by the EC Supplies Directive and the GATT Agreement on Government Procurement

'Warlike' stores (i.e. most categories of defence equipment) are excluded from the arrangements made under the EC Supplies Directive and the GATT Agreement on Government Procurement; but there are still a number of MOD requirements which do not count as 'warlike' and which must be advertised in the *Official Journal of the European Communities*. Purchasing authorities are required to advertise in the *Official Journal* contracts for such items worth more than £110,000 (a threshold which varies from time to time); all suitably qualified firms in the member countries who respond to the advertisement are invited to tender and no discrimination is made between firms on grounds of nationality in the award of contracts. The GATT arrangements are similar and relate to requirements worth more than £92,000 (again subject to variation). Where possible, the MOD is ready to carry out the necessary checks on firms' technical competence and financial standing in time for them to compete for these jobs.

The *Official Journal* is issued almost daily from Luxembourg. Subscriptions can be arranged through HM Stationery Office, 49 High

Holborn, London WC1V 6HB at a cost of £40 to £50 a year. Many chambers of commerce or the larger reference libraries have copies available. The Export Intelligence Service of the British Overseas Trade Board can also provide firms with copies of contract notices appearing in the EC *Official Journal* for those products which the firm produces (and indeed with information on other opportunities overseas).

Annex 2 Contact Points

Contracts Branch/Administration 3
Room 431, St George's Court
Ministry of Defence
14 New Oxford Street
London WC1A 1EJ
01-632 5555 or 5629

Best contact point for general advice on contracts policy and procedure for firms at all stages of seeking MOD business. (Enquiries relating to specific contracts or tenders issued should be addressed to the issuing branch.) Firms interested in direct contracts should approach this branch which will circulate details of their products or services to all interested purchasing areas of the Ministry, including project staff and those concerned with non-equipment items.

Further information can be obtained from the following:

The Society of British Aerospace Companies Limited
29 King Street
St James's
London SW1Y 6RD
01-839 3231

The British Naval Equipment Association
32–8 Leman Street
London E1 8EW
01-488 0171

The Electronic Engineering Association
Leicester House
8 Leicester Street
London WC2H 7BN
01-437 0678

Marketing in Small Businesses

The Electronic Components Industry Federation
7–8 Savile Row
London W1X 1AF
01-437 4127

The Defence Manufacturers Association of Great Britain
136 High Street
Guildford
Surrey GU1 3HL
0483 579333

Case study: Airship Industries [2]

A young British marine engineer, Roger Munk, whose dream was to bring about the commercial rebirth of the British airship industry almost succeeded where many of his predecessors had failed, often with tragic consequences, as they tried to master ligther-than-air flight against more down-to-earth economics. Roger Munk originally set up his airship manufacturing venture in the late 1970s, which was then called Airship Developments Limited and was located at Cardington, birthplace of the ill-fated R101 airship.

Munk had started out backed only by £10,000, his skills as an engineer, and designer and little financial support. He was, however, determined to succeed in manufacturing a working airship which would feature modern technology. Unfortunately, crisis followed crisis, reaching a climax in the winter of 1979. At the time of his first airship's crucial maiden flight, Munk had a record overdraft, creditors pressing, and reports of gloomy weather.

By mid-1984, owing seven million pounds, bankruptcy was staring Roger Munk in the face, and he commented:

> 'We ran out of money, basically; the production programme went ahead on time, the problem is the sales didn't; but the taps were told to be kept open on the production side, and of course as the production went through on time, the cash flow going out of the company went out on time, but the money coming in didn't.'

Their first airship sale was to Japan Airlines for promotional work and the Japanese film manufacturer, Fuji Film, leased an airship for the Olympic Games at Los Angeles. For the first time Airship Industries was able to display their product to a worldwide audience, and significantly, achieve this in an arena dominated by another airship – the Goodyear Blimp. This was the position when Alan Bond, an Australian entrepreneur, baled them out. He saw the potential of the product, that is, airships and their profitable development, but perhaps more significantly, Bond was interested in technical innovation.

Photo copyright: Airship Industries, Ltd.

His new company is the only one in the world making airships to sell, but in 1984 few customers wanted to buy. Bond's stake in Airship Industries of £10 million was an investment which was required to make a return. At this time there were eight airships already flying and seven more being built at Cardington, historical home of Britain's airship industry, and in America. Airship Industries had made quite a departure from the usual airship format. Their airships had vectored propellers, Porsche sports car engines and were built of the latest plastics; these new-technology airships each carried a price tag of over £2 million and the airships were about to win the Certificate of Airworthiness, the only one of its type since the 1930s.

Bond first became interested in airships when he saw the Goodyear Blimp covering the America's Cup Race which his yacht was winning for Australia. Bond was used to winning, and there was nothing sentimental in his approach to the airship company. He commented:

> 'Well I think everyone agrees, it was a total risk, we accepted that as being a risk at the time, but it has the potential to lead the world, and there are very few high-technology products where you can be the number one in the world.'

At Airship Industries, Bond had installed fellow Australian, Alan Birchmore in the Baker Street offices of the company. Birchmore had an impressive record of revitalizing gloomy companies. His strategy was based on sales and leasing. He drafted a master plan for recovery and his short-term priority was cash flow. Airship Industries needed immediate income as the product had to pay its way. A few days later this strategy was implemented. Birchmore had to impress upon the organization *and* its current and potential customers that the turnaround strategy had the probability of being effective.

The Japanese responded immediately by expressing an interest in further advertising work, and leasing was just the kind of short-term deal that Birchmore needed. Fuji's market share was massively increased as a result of the previous leasing contract covering the Olympic Games and they had already shown an interest in long leases in America and South-East Asia. In the short term they were Airship Industries' star customer. At Cardington, Birchmore's team found that the Japanese would not commit themselves. Whatever the Japanese thought of advertising by airship, on the other side of the Atlantic, Goodyear, the major US competitor, did not need this kind of deal.

Goodyear had examined possibilities such as radars tethered at up to 70,000 ft for atmospheric and space use, long endurance anti-submarine missions by blimps towing underwater arrays, and heavy-lift transportation for offshore supplies loading. They had considered several possible blimp missions in detail, with heavy emphasis on cost and comparative economics.

In the early 1980s however the US Navy, and also the Coastguard, became interested in using blimps for various surveillance operations. Either one of these huge concerns had the capacity to generate lucrative business for an airship manufacturer. Goodyear were well placed as they were the traditional domestic supplier and they had the expertise. Goodyear had problems however. Since the 1960s their airship fleet had been scaled down, and they now had only four blimps for public relations work.

In early 1981, Goodyear loaned one of its blimps to the US Coastguard for trials. The experiments seemed to be a success, and for a while, hopes ran high on both sides that a favourable decision might be taken to adopt the airship as an operational craft. However, nothing came of this optimism and confident forecasting, and in the end Goodyear simply could not deliver the goods. The new Airship Industries stepped in where Goodyear left off, and the Coastguard wanted further airship trials, this time fully operational. Bond was confident that the British airships with their vectored thrust propellers and increased lifting capacity could meet the Coastguard's needs, and would thus achieve the breakthrough from small-time advertising to the big league.

Roger Munk's design team had only eight weeks to plan every detail of the Coastguard airship. Every pot of paint, every rivet, every rope had to be evaluated by an American auditor before the Coastguard approved the airship for the 6-month trial. As always with such contracts, specifications are of paramount importance and every detail is strictly checked. This is especially so for a new, untried, and as yet unproven product. Moreover, given the history of the airship, it was hardly surprising that such thoroughness was involved. John Wood, co-founder of Airship Industries and now their top salesman in America had to impress Captain Wallace of the US Coastguard. Captain Wallace headed the team which tested the airship operationally. After these tests were completed, Airship Industries still had to win the deal.

Wood took the Coastguard to see how the airship's special equipment was installed, involving the customer at all stages of the design and building of the prototype. Clearly such a craft had to be purpose-built, given its operational specification. An M60 machine gun, for example, had to be mounted on the side door of the gondola. This was because Wallace's main task for the airship will be tracking down drug smugglers in the Caribbean. Suddenly, just at the time Wallace's team were evaluating the Skyship 600, it became a

Marketing in Small Businesses

one-horse race when Goodyear surprisingly pulled out of the contest for the Coastguard deal. The basic reason was that the final specification would require considerable modification to Goodyear's basic design.

At the US Coastguard's Washington headquarters, negotiations over Airship Industries' price continued into the summer of 1985. For the British company, the trial alone was worth over £2 million.

At this time the US Navy expressed an interest in cheap radar-carrying blimps to support its guided missile fleets. Airship Industries responded immediately stating their willingness to tender for whatever the Navy wished bids for. To give them a US foothold, Airship Industries teamed up with the American electronics giant, Westinghouse, who would provide the Navy blimp's radar. Goodyear responded by allying themselves with two American avionics firms, Sperry and Litton. However, Airship Industries' team claimed an early advantage. Perhaps because of the interest shown by their counterparts in the US Coastguard, Navy officials used a British airship to undertake a series of operational trials in order to evaluate the airship's capabilities at their test centre in Philadelphia. The arrangement was under a leasing agreement which gave Airship Industries a much-needed boost to its cash flow of half a million dollars.

Points of deliberation

- What are the likely problems facing the small company involved in high-technology, high-value product development?
- Given Roger Munk's 'dream', is it likely that an early, thorough market appraisal would have modified his approach to the airship development?
- How exacting were the US Coastguard demands leading to the 6-month trial, and what would be their likely impact on a small company, say, without the backing that Airship Industry enjoyed?
- What supporting links seem to be developing and strengthening Airship Industries' position?
- Is Airship Industries' position seemingly unassailable? (It was noted that the price of Airship Industries' shares had dropped back to 33p in September 1987.)

Notes

1 Extracted from 'Selling to the MOD', Ministry of Defence, 1985.
2 © 1987, P. Murphy.

Further reading

Cabinet Office (MPO) (1984) *Government Purchasing*, London: HMSO.
Forrester, J. (1983) *Selling to the UK Government*, Birmingham: Birmingham Chamber of Industry and Commerce.

11 Franchising

Synopsis

Franchising is an alternative form of distribution strategy, which is designed to give the larger organization a means of rapid market penetration and a wider geographical coverage at relatively low cost. The combination of central purchasing power, local presence, and 'distributor' investment, represents a strong challenge to the more traditional patterns which rely on independent or wholly-owned channels of distribution. As franchisee the small enterprise, in return for financial investment, usually has the benefits of carrying a national trade name, a ready product or service and the support of a complete marketing policy including shop design, packaging, and other promotional support.

Concept of franchising

In one form or another franchising has been with us for a few hundred years, the 'tied-inns' being a classic example. In contemporary terms what exactly constitutes franchising is not too clear, but those organizations we closely associate with the practice such as fast-food and printing services, operate under the business-format system. The British Franchise Association's definition states that 'franchising is a contractual licence granted by one person (the franchisor) to another (the franchisee)'. The terms of the licence:

- Permit the franchisee to carry on a particular business under a specific name belonging to or associated with the franchisor.
- Entitle the franchisor to exercise control during the period of the franchise over the manner in which the franchisee carries on the business.
- Oblige the franchisor to provide the franchisee with assistance in carrying on the business.
- Require the franchisee periodically during the period of the

Franchising

franchise to pay the franchisor sums of money in consideration for the franchise, or for goods and services provided by the franchisor to the franchisee.

Franchising in the United Kingdom

Franchising operations in the UK represented some £2.2 billion in 1987 and accounted for over 90,000 full-time and some 150,000 part-time jobs. These figures represent a growth of over 400 per cent in turnover and 180 per cent in employment over a five-year period, while sales were forecast to reach £6.6 billion by 1991. However, the UK was somewhat behind North America and other European countries, in its commitment to franchising. In the US total sales through franchising represented one-third of all retail sales and amounted to a massive £94 billion pa while in Canada and France, the figures were estimated at £11 billion and £6 billion respectively.

To a large extent, franchising has been encouraged by changing economic, political, and social factors. Redundancy and subsequent government encouragement to business start-ups, have been matched by a greater involvement of financial institutions, including the banks, in providing funds and assistance to both franchisors and franchisees. Additionally, changes in consumer life styles have led to increasing demand for service and convenience of the type that franchises provide.

Opportunities for the potential franchisee

The best-known sector is probably the fast-food business, yet many of the major companies in the sector have been reluctant to expand rapidly through franchising in what has proved to be a fickle competitive market.

This reluctance however appears to be changing. McDonalds, for example, has kept to company-owned outlets in the UK for the past decade, but now it has started to offer franchises. Kentucky Fried Chicken, another of the stalwarts of the fast-food business and one which has been in franchising for several years, and Burger King, which has more than 80 per cent of its 5,000 restaurants world-wide as franchise operations actively seek entrepreneurs and corporate organizations with funds, who believe that the sector will grow rapidly in the late 1980s.

Apart from fast food, another well-established franchise sector is provided by car services. This sector has had its problems over the years, in line with the fluctuations in the UK car market, although it was more stable in 1987. With over 18 million cars on the road in the

UK, there seems to be plenty of scope for growth. In 1987 Hometune claimed to be the world's largest mobile car engine tuning service. Established in 1968, franchises tune more than 180,000 cars a year and new services include Autosheen, a car valeting service carried out at a customer's home or office. The company increased its number of franchisees from 20 to over 100 during 1986 to 1987.

A market research report on franchising pointed out that:

> where a car services franchisor has a sound business format, the franchisee can earn a reasonable living without making a fortune or, where a franchisee already has a strong established business a franchise such as Budget-Rent-A-Car can represent a profitable addition.
>
> (Mintel Retail Intelligence)

Retailing is another growing franchise area, although the UK lags behind other parts of continental Europe. The Benetton fashion chain, for example, has used franchising to expand its operations in Europe.

Convenience foods represent an attractive sector for expansion. Late Supershops, for example, are convenience stores developed by the Co-Operative Wholesale Society. Franchisees benefit from CWS's huge buying power to help sell at competitive prices. Other retailers offer a variety of services. The instant print sector, such as Prontaprint, has grown rapidly, providing a service mainly to business customers. Film developing shops such as Foto Inn have also flourished helped by the growth in tourism both at home and abroad.

New market opportunities are emerging all the time. With over 5 million homes in the UK more than 60 years old, for example, the business opportunities in refurbishing property are a clear growth sector. Gun-Point, a system which repoints buildings, has franchises covering the whole of England and Wales.

The current spread of franchising operations covering such markets as film developing, fashion, fast food, car rental, drain cleaning and printing services, is likely to be greatly expanded in the future. Both existing companies and new entrants are likely to provide increasing opportunities for the would-be smaller enterprise. For example at the time of writing the Abbey National Building Society had announced plans to franchise its Cornerstone estate agency chain and certain shoe manufacturers had actually entered the arena. Likewise, the move towards speciality fashion outlets represents further opportunity for expansion.

Tie-Rack[1]

Lucy Brennan was 'bored, stuck in a rut, and needed a change' when she worked as an account executive in a London advertising agency. So she decided to start up her own business. Ms Brennan, twenty-six decided that her lack of experience in running a small business meant that she should take up a franchise.

She researched various franchise opportunities, with assistance from the British Franchise Association information packs, and decided that 'Tie-Rack outshone the rest of the pack'. Tie-Rack was founded in 1981 by Roy Bishko and, it is claimed, is the world's leading specialist retailer of ties and accessories for men and women. It has some 115 retail outlets, mainly franchised, with plans for a further 40 stores to be opened throughout the UK this year. In June 1987 the company was floated on the stock market and was over-subscribed eighty-five times.

'The flotation has added further impetus to our expansion programme,' says Ron Delnevo, Tie-Rack's franchise director. 'We are looking for people of all ages and from diverse backgrounds who are prepared to make a commitment to the success of the business.'

Ms Brennan had a clear idea of what she wanted from a franchisor: a well defined marketing approach, a quality product, effective back-up, and acceptable margins to generate sufficient profit. 'After a few preliminary meetings we came to understand how Tie-Rack could meet these objectives,' she recalls. 'What became even clearer was the amount of hard work needed in order to make such a venture viable for both parties.'

The cost of Ms Brennan's franchise, which she took up in September 1986, was £52,000. She also has to pay Tie-Rack 22.5 per cent of her turnover, out of which Tie-Rack pays rent, rates and service charges. Tie-Rack owns the lease of her shop in Ealing, West London. 'When you become your own boss, the buck stops with you and no one else.' Ms Brennan points out. 'Being a franchisee means the buck still stops with you on most things, but I also have the support and back-up of the Tie-Rack network, drawing on their experience and expertise.'

She believes that one of the most important factors in the franchisor/franchisee relationship – which can often be strained – is an open communications system with encouragement to share news and views. 'Our Tie-Rack area manager is our main linchpin to the central operation,' Ms Brennan explains. 'He or she becomes supporter, teacher, motivator, colleague, and often friend.'

On a more practical level, Tie-Rack's 30-day merchandise system is seen by Ms Brennan as a crucial element in making the franchise work. 'We can return any merchandise not sold to Tie-Rack for full credit, and it enables us to merchandise our shop effectively without tying up our finances in slow selling stock,' she says. 'What is good stock for one area may not work for another, so stock rotation and redistribution is a benefit for the system.'

Ms Brennan remains enthusiastic about franchising: 'I love being a franchisee, although there are times when I hate it too – especially when I am installing the January sale at 11.30 pm on Christmas Eve,' she says. 'But then you love it when the doors open and people flood in to snap up bargains.' Her success in the first year has encouraged her to plan setting up a second franchise soon.

Financing the franchise

All the major clearing banks have a keen interest in franchising, and are willing to offer finance for new schemes.

Nat West lays claim to being the first British bank to appoint a manager to deal solely with franchising – way back in July 1981. The bank now has three franchise managers with a support team of four other staff. The Nat West approach is to provide detailed information packages as a basic guide to franchising for both customers and branch managers. The bank's major concern with advancing money to any small business venture – including franchising – is the high failure rate among small businesses in general.

An estimated mortality rate for small businesses in the first year would be of the order of 25 per cent, and for failures in the first five years, estimates suggest the failure rate varies between 40 and 70 per cent. But of all new franchises, the worst estimate for one year failure is 10 per cent. Lloyds Bank claims that 8 per cent is nearer the mark and that if non-members of the British Franchise Association are excluded, the failure rate in the first year drops to 2 per cent. Banks' policies vary but as a general rule of thumb they will contribute anything between 30 and 70 per cent of the start-up money required – with the rest coming from savings, sale of assets, a second mortgage, friends or relatives.

Franchisees short of their own capital or security may persuade a bank to back them under the government's Loan Guarantee Scheme. This gives the lender a government guarantee for 70 per cent of the loan which can be claimed if the borrower cannot repay.

Oasis
Raising finance to enable her to buy a franchise was one of the major hurdles faced by Jackie Brierton when she decided to open an Oasis fashion retailing franchise in Edinburgh two years ago. She recalls:

'Although I had previously run my own retail business with some degree of success, the banks were still wary of the single business woman set-up. It simply amazed me. There was at that time – and still is to a certain extent – a very large gap in the fashion franchise market. I was basically asking for an overdraft facility of £12,000 to open a fashion outlet in one of the most fashion-conscious cities in the UK.'

Ms Brierton, who had previously run her own newsagent shop in Scotland, decided that running a low-margin and long-hour-type of operation such as a confectioner-tobacconist-newsagent was not for her. 'I had always been interested in fashion and also thought it a good idea to become involved with a successful chain through franchising,' she explains.

She therefore paid a visit to the 1984 National Franchise Exhibition where she met the Oasis team. Oasis is a High Street fashion chain with thirty branches throughout the UK which is keen to expand through franchising. 'There are few people offering a good, comprehensive, but flexible fashion franchise package,' she believes. 'I liked the options that Oasis could offer me – they had a good style and image that I knew would work in the Edinburgh retail environment.'

Ms Brierton eventually persuaded her bank manager to lend her the money and, with a total investment of £35,000, opened her first store in Edinburgh in an upmarket shopping centre development. Earlier this year she opened her second store, this time in Glasgow, and now employs eighteen staff (nine full-time) to run the two branches.

Points to consider

Franchising offers many of the advantages of running a business – such as job satisfaction and independence – without many of the problems that lead to the high failure rates associated with small enterprises. The aspiring franchisee should address a number of basic questions and evaluate all possible options before finally taking action:

Marketing in Small Businesses

- *Self-motivation.* Objectively assess the motivation behind the decision to go for franchising. Consider the emotional stamina needed to cope with working longer and/or unsocial hours in order to establish the business.
- *Type of franchise.* Consider capital required for the different types of franchise and the types of operation that appeal most. For example around £10,000 would be needed for a low-cost cleaning franchise while a minimum of £150,000 would be required for a food franchise such as Pizza Express. Deliberate on time demands, e.g. being on constant call (drain cleaning), long hours (fast food), normal working day (printing).
- *The franchisor.* Consider management ability, integrity and financial stability. How long in business and what policies and plans for development. If possible, contact existing franchisees to check on level of support given and any problem areas. Carefully evaluate terms and conditions.

In the final analysis the quality of service provided to the end-user will largely depend on the effectiveness of the franchisee. Comprehensive franchisor marketing support may bring in the customers, but it is up to the franchisee to provide the satisfaction that will lead to repeat purchasing of the service.

Case study: Olivers[2]

The unique Olivers concept of wholesome, fresh food and immaculate service has been developed over a number of years, and lends itself admirably to franchising.

Hot bread shops were opened initially in Scotland in 1977 – and such was the popularity of the wholesome, fresh, Olivers product that the chain quickly expanded. In 1982 a coffee shop was added to the shop in Stirling creating the first Olivers coffee shop and bakery. Later in the same year the first franchised Olivers opened. In 1987, 11 of the 30 Olivers outlets were franchised.

As the chain expanded south, coffee shop and take-away sales grew rapidly, and in 1987 the bread shop contributed on average, less than a quarter of total sales. The growth of sales generated by the opening of new Olivers bread and coffee shops since 1982 has been matched by an impressive growth per outlet.

Olivers is operating in a vibrant, expanding market, and year after year its shops enjoy growth which, in real terms, is well ahead of inflation. Existing franchised Olivers coffee shops and bakery outlets have enjoyed an average rate of growth of 15 per cent per annum between 1983 and 1986. Olivers is more than just the provision of

Olivers – St David's Link, Cardiff (Photo copyright: Olivers (UK) Ltd, Bedford, 1988)

Marketing in Small Businesses

quality bread, sandwiches and other appetizing foods. It is a combination of ambience, service, and value for money which adds up to a pleasurable eating experience. The concept is designed to complement and take the chores out of, town centre shopping.

George Dewar, from Kirkcaldy, Scotland, started a franchise in Kirkcaldy High Street in 1985. His sister and her husband were already in the fast-food business, as franchisees for Olivers in Elgin, Scotland – an operation which had been going since 1982.

Armed with his redundancy money and life savings, Mr Dewar was able to find about 30 per cent of the £240,000 needed to set up an Olivers outlet. He prepared a business plan, with the help of Olivers, and approached three banks – National Westminster, Barclays, and the ICFC. Nat West impressed him the most and he was able to obtain a capital loan from it, backed with a guarantee from the government's small business scheme.

Although Olivers offers a range of specialist services for franchisees, such as surveyors and interior designers, Mr Dewar first decided to go it alone when planning the new store. However, afraid of hidden costs from doing it himself, he eventually decided to use the expertise of Olivers to set the store up.

They opened in March 1985 with 24 staff, both part-time and full-time, who were given pre-opening training by Olivers. The initial product range was soon extended by Mr Dewar who found that in his area, demand for cream cakes was especially high. Points such as these, and new recipes and ideas, are exchanged by all franchisees at regular meetings at Olivers head office.

Mr Dewar's business took off, exceeding sales targets by 20 per cent in both 1986 and 1987 and he had planned to add another 50 seats to his 129 seat coffee shop section. Although a Wimpy fast food operation opened next door to him, Mr Dewar maintained that this had not affected his business since they were in different markets. However, just to make sure, he considered spreading his risk by opening another franchised outlet in Dunfermline.

Points for deliberation

- What element of Olivers marketing mix appears to be somewhat different from that found in most franchise operations?
- George Dewar considers Olivers and Wimpy to operate in different markets. Which segments of the market are these franchises likely to appeal to and what different needs are being met?
- What pricing strategy is likely to be most effective for an operation of this nature?

- What form of local promotion, if any, would be needed to stimulate growth and what factors limit expansion?

Notes

1 *Financial Times* 28 September 1987 (reproduced by kind permission of Financial Times Ltd).
2 Source: Olivers HQ, Bedford and *Financial Times* 28 September 1987.

Further reading

'Franchising survey', *Financial Times*, 28 September 1987.
Curran, J. (1978) 'Franchising at the Crossroads', *Marketing*, April.
Golzen, G. and Barrow, C. (1983) *Taking up a Franchise*, London: Kogan Page.
Mendelsohn, M. (1987), *The Guide to Franchising*, Oxford: Pergamon Press.

12 Marketing high technology

Synopsis

In the field of high technology the smaller enterprise is very often faced with acute uncertainty concerning internal developments and external reactions. Having experienced various levels of success and failure in coping with the financial structure and product research and development, the enterprise faces the daunting task of actually reaching the market and invariably having to overcome stiff resistance. There are however, a number of courses of action which the enterprise can take in order to reduce this resistance, among which is building an image of credibility.

Importance of company image

Fostering a favourable image, which is to a large extent reflective of customer needs, has been stressed throughout the text, but it is perhaps more important in a high-technology environment, where the customer will invariably need to place a good deal of faith in the supplier's claims, due to the risk and uncertainty involved in the purchasing decision. The customer's perception of the firm's ability to deliver on time, the quality of its products, the level of after-sales service, its ability to survive over the long term, and its resolve to keep up with technological change, will enhance, or diminish its capability image. In this respect, it is vital that the firm communicates such attributes to the market in a logical and effective manner.

The communications strategy should attempt to strengthen the enterprise's position by focusing on those issues which add to its credibility image, such as financial backing, any existing important customers, links with research institutions and distributorship agreements, if appropriate. Otherwise, the smaller high-technology enterprise will be at a considerable disadvantage relative to its larger competitors who have the benefit of an established reputation.

Need for customer reassurance

In a fast-changing technological environment with many suppliers vying for business, it is inevitable that customers will face an abundance of claims about product superiority while coping with the problem of relatively rapid product obsolescence. Often the customer may be confused with the bombardment of claims and as such, a primary need will be that of reassurance regarding the successful outcome of any purchase agreement reached. The supplier should therefore attempt to eliminate or reduce doubt in the mind of the customer and this approach should be a conscious development of the total marketing strategy. In the following case the customer, a non-technical person, is faced with the task of selecting a suitable supplier.

Company secretary

'I had eight separate proposals to deal with. Give or take the odd differences, most of the suppliers were saying much the same thing, including many technical factors I just didn't understand. Frankly, few of the proposals gave me any confidence regarding the viability of the companies. In conversations with the various technical representatives most seemed determined to knock the competition rather than concentrate on what I wanted to hear. For example: "Why should we choose their particular company?" In the end we decided on supplier X. They had the name and the reputation and considering the amount of capital expenditure involved, I just couldn't take the risk of choosing one of the lesser-known suppliers, even though I was impressed by some of their equipment demonstrations.'

Conclusion

Clearly in this case the order was decided on the basis of supplier image and reputation. There was no guarantee that the company had made the best possible purchase relative to their requirements, but at least the company secretary could sleep easily in the knowledge that the chosen supplier had credibility. Demonstrations of products, performance were obviously not enough and it would seem that technical representation left a lot to be desired.

Building an acceptable image

Financial backing

With a high-risk development there will often be a necessity to convince interest groups other than the ultimate end-users of the product. For example, in raising finance for new-products development, potential investors will need to have a high level of confidence regarding the viability of the venture as with organizations within the marketing chain (such as distributors), when the product is due for launch. Companies without a track record will obviously have difficulties in raising the necessary capital, therefore preparing a good case is essential as the following extract demonstrates.

> The rapid advance of new technology has, to a certain extent, placed banks in an embarrassing position. How can the local bank manager be assured that the technical side of the proposition is feasible?
>
> To get around this Barclays has set up various connections with government and technical bodies which can appraise the viability of new-technology products.
>
> However, even the comfort of a technical appraisal is not, in itself sufficient. Is there a market for the product? Does the product meet the needs of the market? Can the business sell the product?
>
> It is a fact that the majority of problems arise because companies fail to pay sufficient regard to the marketing considerations.[1]

If the enterprise is successful in obtaining the necessary financial support this in itself is a start to building credibility. It is a fact that success breeds success and awareness of such backing should help to raise confidence in the market place.

Third-party links

Establishing connections with other business parties particularly if the latter are already successful and known to some extent – can further help build credibility. Such relationships will often prove mutually beneficial as they will not only represent a good promotional opportunity but also may provide a means of cost-sharing developments. In the following case comments from a major customer of the third party help to boost the enterprises' image.

> Peter Manly and co-director John Walker (Logic Computing Systems) are promoting an up-market suite of ledger software written by David Jarman, the managing director of Jarman

Accounts Software. Manly states; 'You can, with this software, set up budgets for whole departments. It's not just another visible record system that just keeps track of the accounts but a whole budget system, very much geared towards management accountants and management accounting. The Sirius and IBM Personal Computer (PC) are going to appear a lot more in the business market place so Jarman ledger software is going to appeal to a lot more businesses in the future.'

Manly's remarks were validated by David Press, the group accountant for Green Shield and its associated companies. Press told *Computing*: 'This software is terrific and we are using it in quite a substantial way. Logic told us that the Jarman system would run everything for us and it does just that.'[2]

This was obviously good publicity for both companies and would no doubt have provided an excellent talking point for their respective sales representatives.

Sometimes, co-operative ventures with respected dominant firms are possible and awareness of any such arrangement is likely to enhance the firm's market presence and reduce barriers to entry. For example, IBM's personal computers have been well supported with software packages provided by small, independent software houses and this has been to the advantage of both sides. While the smaller enterprises have benefitted from IBM's marketing strength, IBM's products have had the advantage of wide-ranging software support; a classic case of symbiosis – the principle of two entities depending upon each other for survival.

Use of trade and business media

Business and technical media such as trade and professional journals and the quality newspapers, represent very credible sources of communication. If the enterprise believes it has a product development worth a write-up, then every effort should be made to use these channels. However, unless the product is revolutionary, it is unlikely that such reporting will be very effective unless other, favourable attributes regarding the enterprise are included – for example, reputable financial backers and third-party links, as mentioned previously. In this way there is more to say about the enterprise relative to what customers would wish to know about a potential supplier and of course, it helps to build the former's confidence in the latter, given the knowledge that other organizations have demonstrated their faith in the enterprise.

This build-up to customer targeting should be developed

systematically and with a degree of patience. The enterprise should attempt to build strength upon strength and in the end, have much more to communicate than just technical know-how and/or an attractive product.

Word-of-mouth influences

Once initial custom has been obtained it is important to consider the likely influence of information spreading by word-of-mouth. It is probably far more beneficial in the long term, to spend time and effort ensuring complete satisfaction of these initial customers, than to channel all available effort towards increasing market penetration. Bad news tends to travel fast whereas good news communicated by word-of-mouth can be far more influential than the best advertising campaigns. New customer contacts will sometimes seek references from existing users via various means such as through professional channels or say by requesting a demonstration at a user site. It is not difficult to understand that any adverse comments arising out of such contact could virtually ruin all chances of doing business with the prospective customers. Favourable word-of-mouth communication is also likely to result in prospective customers seeking out the enterprise without any prompting from the latter.

This channel of influence is difficult to define and analyse with any degree of accuracy but it suffices to say that it exists and it is not insignificant in its contribution to the success, image, and reputation of the enterprise. Many business experts believe that industrial organizations behave much like consumers when adopting new and innovative products. That is, only a very small percentage of the market will be prepared to adopt initially, while the remainder will adopt in a progressive manner, as evidence of the success of the product builds up over time. It is also considered that this 'evidence' is largely generated by a satisfactory word-of-mouth communication originating from these innovators or early adopters who may themselves be opinion leaders and thus, very influential. However, they may be difficult to identify for purposes of specific targetting, as they are not all large organizations.

Developing a marketing framework

In summary the key to effective marketing rests on the acceptance of an in-built market resistance and uncertainty and a determination on the part of the enterprise to do as much as possible to break down these barriers in a systematic and patient manner. It also requires the recognition that product research and development will invariably have its uncertainties and that careful thought must be given to planning R and D programmes and to methods of financing. It is on the success of these early stages of development that the high-technology enterprise can begin to develop effective market positioning, similar to that described in Fig 12.1

Any attempt to short-circuit the communications process is likely to dilute the impact on the market. For example, the mere reporting via the business press of some new product development may fall on deaf ears unless there is more to add in the way of credible sources of third-party co-operation, provisional distribution agreement, and other newsworthy items.

Case study: Celltech[3]

Britain's leading biotechnology specialist company, Celltech has its headquarters in Slough, Berkshire. Its managers have a knack for illuminating scientific mysteries to the layman – in particular, two fundamental discoveries of the 1970s on which all its work is based. DNA is the process of transforming cells into a miniature chemical manufacturing plant: transfer, for example, a strip of DNA carrying the instruction code for making human insulin into an E.*coli* cell, and this humble bacterium dutifully produces natural insulin in a way that nature, unaided, would not. Broadly speaking, it is this technology which could have long term implications for the process industries: food, chemicals, energy, and waste treatment.

Cell hybridization, on the other hand, actually creates a minuscule protein factory: fuse an antibody-producing cell with a tumour cell, which replicates endlessly, and the result is a non-stop production line for antibodies. Derived from a single fused cell (hence, monoclonal), these antibodies are exquisitely pure and minutely specific in their recognition of foreign substances, such as viruses or bacteria, invading the body. Impossible to obtain in bulk by traditional commercial methods, they are invaluable not only in early diagnosis and therapy without side-effects, but in the advance of medical understanding – the basis for future prevention and cure. Celltech explained the 'company mission': 'We intend to stick to these two new biotechnology processes, to establish major profitable business in defined markets, and to commercialize ideas arising in the academic community,' stated Chief Executive Gerald Fairtlough.

There had been major technical advances in both the pharmaceutical and the industrial fields of biotechnology – but these had been achieved by large companies, like ICI and G.D. Searle, who were able to support research investment from their other profit-making business. Investors in companies that specialize in

Target Audience	Financial Community	Potential 3rd Party Ventures	Market Middlemen	Market Innovators	Initial Customers	Other Market Segments
Main Channel of Communication	Personal	Technical/Trade Press	Business Press	Personal and Non-personal	Personal	Word-of-Mouth
Main Message Theme	Quality and Commitment of Management + Viability of Venture	+ Financial Backing	+ Progress/Technical Expertise + Market Potential	+ Technical Innovation	+ Reassurance	= Capability Image
Enterprise Activity	Business Plan	R and D Programme	Prototype Development	Selective Launch	Develop and Sustain Customer Satisfaction	Develop Wider Market

Market Development Over Time

Figure 12.1 Marketing framework: build-up of capability image

Marketing high technology

Celltech's new 2,000 litre fermenter gives the company a total fermentation capacity in excess of 5,000 litres, consolidating its position as the world's leading manufacturer of monoclonal antibodies. (Photo by Infopress Ltd, London.)

biotechnology alone, by contrast, needed all the promised developments in health care their chosen companies could muster if they were to live long enough to enjoy a return.

For example, Cetus, the American firm, was founded in 1971 and rocketed to financial fame in 1980, when its initial public offering on the US stock exchange fetched a record $120 million. Pre-tax profit for 1983–4 was a mere $1.06 million, and earnings per share for the first quarter of fiscal 1985 only $0.02. Biogen, founded in the late 1970s by Nobel prizewinner Walter Gilbert, reported a turnover of $22 million for the first nine months of last year – and a net loss of $10.9 million. Even 9-year old Genetech, the acknowledged world leader, with a fairly hefty turnover in 1984 of $67 million, achieved profits of only around $3 million – hardly startling for a company with a market capitalization of $600 million.

Celltech itself could be excused its overall losses in 1984, down by 5 per cent to £1.9 million (on a turnover which increased by 125 per cent to £1.86 million). The company was formed only in 1980, and the heavy investment of the early years had been written off and not capitalized. But given Celltech's nature, not only as a specialist company, but as a very small specialist and given the experience of more established specialists so far, what hope would Celltech have of turning biotech into a profitable business?

Gerald Fairtlough believed that the economic impact of genetic engineering would ultimately be analogous to that of the semiconductor; but he pointed out that: 'We're only 10 years into the discoveries of recombinant DNA and cell fusion.' No commentator had ever predicted that the real impact on industrial microbiology, which is where the billion dollar business might lie (an estimated $25 billion in petrochemicals, for example), might start to be felt before the very end of the century. The enormous potential for improving crop strains through genetic engineering seemed promising, although this was an area which Celltech itself had shunned because of the 'different techniques involved, and the need for greenhouses and the like'.

Success for a biotechnology specialist, maintained Celltech, depended partly on a careful balance between short- and long-term projects. For a small company, with no money to burn, success also required judicious juggling with the commercial strategies of contract research, joint ventures licensing and product sales. Most important, perhaps, was a meticulous selection of targets. Major projects in the past – like ICI's development of single-cell protein or the various attempts to turn biomass into a source of energy – had failed (at mighty cost) not for technical reasons, but because they were ill-timed and ill-chosen. Who needed single-cell protein when soya beans are cheap? And what's the point of biomass when oil prices are falling?

Celltech's major work in industrial microbiology had been the successful cloning and expression of the chymosin (rennin) gene in bacteria. The market for rennet in cheese-making was some $70 million annually, and the current source (calves) was vulnerable – so the project, although it turned out more difficult than expected, was an obvious choice but also other companies, like Dow Chemicals, Genetech, and Genex, had unfortunately chosen it, too.

Celltech's early years according to research director Norman Carey, brought a 'reasonable number of research contracts in small investigative areas' which were 'financially small, but very successful'. Rather than diffuse the activities of the parent company into too many disparate directions, in November 1984 Celltech launched its industrial microbiology offshoot, Apcel, a 50:50 joint venture with the US industrial gas and cryogenic plant company, Air Products.

Apcel was involved in the development of potentially heavyweight but longer-term business, running its own risk project on enhanced oil recovery. The combine had thirty Ph.D.s working on research by mid 1985, building up to fifty eventually – roughly double the number similarly engaged elsewhere. 'But of course this will have to be balanced by market pull,' explained Brian Street, Apcel's Chief Executive.

Boots-Celltech was an offshoot company which grew out of the former's diagnostics division in August 1983. Like Apcel, it was a 50:50 joint venture. The partnership with Boots was intended to bring not only necessary finance, but also the older company's reputation and knowledge of the market – essential when Boots-Celltech came into competition with diagnostics giants like Abbott. 'But even if it weren't necessary to have joint ventures,' explained Fairtlough, 'we would still have companies budding off': for while being small has its obvious disadvantages, Fairtlough believed strongly that small is beautiful when seeking innovation and intimate collaboration between scientist and marketer.

This was one factor which all Celltech managers stressed as a vital ingredient in biotech success. 'That way,' commented John Berriman, manager of the culture products division which, with health-care therapy, remains Celltech's core-business, 'you don't get scientists making products at a price nobody will pay, or the men from marketing asking scientists for products nobody could make anyway.' Offshoot companies enabled Celltech simultaneously to stay small (with around 220 staff, one-third of them Ph.D.s), and to grow. Their separate identities were reinforced by the alliances with outside partners.

Celltech's products included a protein hormone assay for thyroid function, which did the work of three previous tests at lower cost and

Marketing in Small Businesses

had entered a £50 million market worldwide; a diagnostic test for chlamydia, an infectious disease which attacks the genital tracts of around a million women annually in the UK alone (and where early diagnosis is important); interferon assay kits, used for early detection of disease as well as for monitoring patients' response to therapy.

Diagnostic products have the advantage of short regulatory procedures. With therapeutic products, however, it may take eight to ten years between conception and marketing, both because of the complexity of the research and because of the rigorous and lengthy regulatory process: Genetech's launch of its human insulin within six years was possible because the genetic structure and the effects of insulin were known from the start (so, again, a wise choice for first product).

Celltech only entered into health care seriously in 1982. It did not expect to launch its products until 1991 – which is why this division had been balanced by culture products, where sales of blood grouping reagents, anti-interferon assays and, most important, monoclonal antibodies were in full swing. Turnover in this group approached £1 million in 1984, Genetech's head start had, however, been a major challenge for Celltech. 'We had to consider,' explained Carey, 'whether or not to enter the health-care business at all because, until our paths diverged, whatever point we reached, Genetech would be five years ahead.' Indeed, when the company was born, one familiar lament was that it gave not only 'too little', but came 'too late'.

Celltech's first task in overcoming the disadvantages of late entry was 'to establish scientific credibility'. Here, the company started with a unique advantage: first option on all discoveries in rDNA and cell hydbridization from the Medical Research Council (MRC), in whose famous Cambridge laboratory for molecular biology Milstein and Kohler had done their Nobel prizewinning work on monoclonal antibodies. At the end of 1983, this agreement was changed, so that Celltech retained exclusive rights to research it had funded directly, and first option rights only where it had been, or would soon be, active in commercializing MRC work. The change was made, commented Dr Bronwen Loder, the assistant director of the LMB, because 'Celltech found its feet very quickly': like the reduction in the stake of the National Enterprise Board (now Technology Group) from 44 per cent to 28 per cent, with a further diminution forthcoming, it was a sign that Celltech was growing up.

Continuing good relations with the MRC meant that Celltech had access to some 1,100 top researchers. It had also built up its own links with university laboratories in the UK and abroad, and had an advisory Science Council studded with fellows of the Royal Society. Celltech's own in-house team of 'entrepreneurial scientists', as Carey described them, were chosen for expertise in their fields and for industrial experience. Carey himself, for example, had been 'heavily responsible' for leading G.D. Searle into rDNA, his team being the first to clone and express the influenza gene in bacteria. Sensibly, recruitment was limited to one appointment a week. The cautious approach helped Celltech to avoid the fate of Biogen, which had laid off 13 per cent of its staff after initial over-expansion in 1985.

To catch up in the biotechnology race, the company had to establish areas of uniqueness, whether technically, in developing expertise in cell culture, for example, or in offering marginal advantages over rival products. Determined also to become more than a middleman between academia and the larger companies, Celltech brought out its first (unique) products in its first year: two anti-interferon antibodies, used in the purification and assay of interferon (Celltech decided against trying for interferon itself, partly because of the competition). It successfully scaled up production of two blood-grouping reagents – a real technical achievement, although for a small market of £7.5 million worldwide.

Most important, it had won the world lead in the bulk production of monoclonal antibodies, which had a potential world market of £150 million. The advantages of its product, based on mammalian cell tissue culture, over those of its rivals seemed more than marginal. Hybritech's product was contaminated mice antibodies, and required vast quantities of mice (20,000 for 1 kg).

In 1984, Celltech invested in a 1,000 litre fermenter, to increase production to 5 kg annually (Hybritech, for comparison, achieves only 1 kg). The decision to enlarge capacity was made with characteristic prudence. 'We estimated the world market, decided on a large share, and then,' says Fairtlough, 'divided by five'.

To establish itself in health care, Celltech tried to balance projects unique to itself (whether for 'scientific kudos' or marketing potential – and still secret) with targets shared by other companies. Human growth hormone to treat dwarfism was a good starter for biotechnology companies: there was an £80 million market, the molecular structure was known and the advantage over the existing product (extracted from human cadavers) was apparent.

The major challenge facing Celltech (and all biotechnology specialists) was finding the correct path towards becoming an integrated, fully fledged business. Health care involves huge investment sums, particularly in the last stages of product development – the clinical trials and regulatory procedures. Celltech had accordingly licensed its growth hormone to Seronon Laboratories Inc. and four of its products (including two for cancer therapy) to Sankyo, Japan's second largest pharmaceutical company. For a small company with limited resources, it had gone as far down the marketing path as was prudent.

Celltech was aware of other future problems both scientific and commercial. Health-care projects, for example, become increasingly difficult to identify. Patents, of vital importance among competitors for the same targets, are a cloudy and possibly contentious area. Also would the large pharmaceutical companies, so far relatively indifferent towards biotechnology (and towards MRC research), change their attitudes, and overtake – or take over – Celltech's work?

Points for deliberation

- What is Celltech's business definition?
- What are the particular problems of the market?
- What are the problems of product development?
- What third-party connections has Celltech established?
- How has Celltech segmented the market?
- How would you describe Celltech's 'credibility image' and how has this been developed?
- What is Celltech's position in the market?

Notes

1 Virgo, P. and Duffel, I. (1983) 'Finding the backing for high-tech start-up firms', *Computing*, September, 18–19.
2 Sederal, A. (1984) 'Accounting has come of age on the micro', *Computing*, 4 April, 30.
3 Extracted from *Management Today*, March 1985 (by kind permission of Haymarket Publications Ltd).

Further reading

'Strategies for growth in high-technology companies', Barclays Bank plc (publication series).
McKenna, R. (1985) *The Regis Touch*, Reading, Mass.: Addison Wesley.
'Promoting innovation in smaller firms', Confederation of British Industry, January, 1988.

Index

AE 62
Abbey National Building Society 198
Acorn Computers 24
Adcock, Paul 177–9
advertising 137–8
aid to small enterprises: information 7–9, 51–2; Loan Guarantee Scheme 201; overseas marketing 156–8, 167–9; product development 91–2
Airship Industries 190–4
Almo-Cut 177–9
Amplivision 110
Apcel 214
Arcady Restaurant 103–4
Argus Software 139–41
Arncliffe Materials Handling 119–20
Arncliffe Tools Ltd 92–4
Automated Scanning Systems (ASS) 164–5
Autosheen 198

Bank of England, and house prices 54–5
Barclays Bank 200
Bejam 60
Bema Ltd 170–2
Benetton 198
Berriman, John 215
Biogen 213
Blauvelt, Euan 159
Bond, Alan 190–3

Booker McConnell 150
branding 90
British Franchise Association 196
British Naval Equipment Association 189
British Overseas Trade Board (BOTB) 9, 156–8, 167–9
British Rail 25
Building Societies Association (BSA) 54
Burger King 197
Butterfingers 10–15
buyer *see* customer

Camford Drives 22
Carey, Norman 214–15
Carr, Chris 77
Carter & Simpson 37–8
Celltech 210–17
Cetus 213
chains, marketing 47–9
Chem-Tech Laboratory Supplies 106–7
communications 128–54: buyer needs and behaviour 133–5; case study: W. Jordan (Cereals) 146–54; channels 135–8; high technology marketing 208–10; interpersonal 135–7, 210; logical approach 129–30; message design and communicator 138–43; need for 128; objectives 129–33; planning 143–5; strategy 130–3

219

Marketing in Small Businesses

competition 35–9: analysis of 38–9
competitor–oriented pricing 107–8
Computer and Office Products (COP) Ltd 43–4
Congdon, Tim 55
Connolly, Jane 10–15
contracts: government 185–7: branch administration 185, conditions 186, financing 187, principles and types of 185–6, quality assurance 187; overseas 169–72
controls, marketing plan 69–70
Co-operative Wholesale Society (CWS) 198
cost of marketing 27–30
CroxMills Pre-packed Meats 117–19
Cum-free Beds 28–30
customer: buying behaviour 39–44; needs and behaviour 133–5; needs identification 19–20; -oriented pricing 107–8; reassurance 207; satisfaction 1, 18–19

David, Cakes of Distinction 15–17
DEFCONS 187
Defence, Ministry of (MOD) 181–8; contracts 185–7; organization and contact points 182–4, 189–90
Defence Manufacturers Association of Great Britain 190
demand, estimating 66–7, 89–90
Derwent Valley Foods 98–100
design, product 90
Dewar, George 204–5
differentiation, product 108–9
distribution 117–26: case study: Strida Ltd 123–6; decision 121–2; evaluation 122–3; problems 117–21
distributors 47–9
Donohoe, Desmond 31–4
Donprint 30–4
Durlacher, Jennifer 159

economy, national 49–51

Economy Energy Systems 121
Electronic Components Industry Federation 190
Electronic Engineering Association 189
Enterprise Initiative 7–9
environment, marketing 35–63: case studies: house prices 52–6, industrial manufacturing and marketing 56–63; competition 35–9; customer behaviour 39–44; government, the public, the economy 49–51; suppliers, retailers, distributors 47–9; technology 44–6
European Community (EC) 9, 188–9
Evans, Karen 10–15
Export Intelligence Service (EIS) 168
exporting *see* overseas marketing

Fairtlough, Gerald 211, 213–15
Field Engineering Ltd 44–5
financing: franchising 200–1; government contracts 187; new product development 208
Fire-Mann (Sales) Ltd 95–8
forecasting, demand 66–7
franchising 196–205: case study: Olivers 202–5; concept of 196–7; financing 200–1; opportunities 197–200; in the UK 197
Frost, Lindsay 150

General Agreement on Tariffs and Trade (GATT) 188–9
Genetech 213
Gill, Keith 98
government: and marketing 49–51: aid and information for small enterprises 51–2, 91–2, Enterprise Initiative 7–9, Loan Guarantee Scheme 201, overseas marketing 156–7, 167–9; marketing to 180–94:

220

Index

case study: Airship Industries 190–4, contact points 189–90, contract conditions 186, contract financing 187, contracts branch administration 185, 189, EC and GATT 188–9, market entry 184–5, MOD 181–8, principles and types of contract 185–6, problems 180–1, quality assurance 187

high technology marketing 206–17: case study: Celltech 210–17; customer reassurance 207; image building 208–9; image, importance of 206; marketing framework 209–10
Hoover Ltd 81–2
house prices 52–6
Howie, Robert 75–7
Hy-Tran Engineering 160, 162–3

IBM 61
ICI Paints 60
image: building 24–5, 208–9; importance in high technology marketing 206
industrial manufacturing and marketing 56–63
inflation 50, 52
Information Processing Systems 39–41
information for small enterprises 5–9, 51–2: overseas marketing 156–8
Ingson Autobodies 107–8
international marketing *see* overseas marketing
interpersonal communication 135–7, 210

JCB 60
Jaguar 60–1
Jarman Accounts Software 208–9
Jordan, Bill 149–51
Jordan, David 150
Jordan, W., (Cereals) 146–54

Kalma Co. 170–2
Kentucky Fried Chicken 197
Kirk, Ray 33
Knowles, Roger and Kathleen 172–7

launch, new product 91
Lee, Graham 150–2
Linn Products 111–15
Lloyds Bank 200
Loan Guarantee Scheme 201
Loder, Dr Bronwen 216
Logic Computing Systems 208–9

MOD *see* Defence, Ministry of
MacCarfrae, David and Hilda 15–17
McCullough, Roy 114
McDonalds 197
McGhee, Kay 98
McKechnie, Roger 98–100
Manpower Services Commission 92
manufacturing industry, and marketing 56–63
market share 68–9
marketing 1–2, 18–19: case studies: Butterfingers 10–15, David, Cakes of Distinction 15–17, Donprint 30–4; communications 128–54; cost 27–30; customer needs identification 19–20; definition 18–19; and distribution 117–26; environment 35–63; franchising 195–205; to government 180–94; high technology 206–17; image building 24–5; orientation 18–34; and other business functions 20–1; overseas 155–79; planning 64–78; and pricing 102–15; products and services 79–100; and selling 26–7; and small enterprises 4–9
Marks & Spencer 25
Marshall, Paul 125
Martin, Bill 55
Merrydown Cider 73–8

221

Marketing in Small Businesses

Metal Component Supplies (MCS) 48–9
Mintel Retail Intelligence 198
Morrisons (Meats) Ltd 143–5
Mossop, Caroline 14
Munk, Roger 190–3

National Westminster Bank 200
new product: development 84–7; pricing 104–5
Newbold Kitchens 26–7
Newitt, Mike 77

Oasis 201
objectives, marketing 67–8: communications 129–33
Olivers 202–5
overseas marketing 155–79: case studies: lmo-Cut 177-9, Woods of Windsor 172–7; contracts 169–72; decision 155–6; documentation 166–7; entry mode 158–60; help and advice 167–9; information sources 156–8; opportunity 163–5; problems 160–3; selection of market 158; UK exporters 161

Pantronic Ltd 166–7
Pike, John 98
planning marketing 64–78: case study: Merrydown Cider 73–8; communications 143–5; controls 69–70; demand forecasting 66–7; formal approach to 64–5; long term 70–2; market share 68–9; objective setting 67–8; strategy 68
Pollak, Mike 77
positioning, product 87–9
Precision Engineering Services 5–6
pricing 102–15: case study: Linn Products 111–15; competitor- and customer-oriented 107–8; factors affecting price 102–4; going-rate 109–10; new product 104–5; policy 105–7; and

product differentiation 108–9
product differentiation 108–9
product life cycle (PLC) 79–84
products and services 79–100: case studies: Derwent Valley Foods 98–100, Fire-Mann (Sales) Ltd 95–8; demand and profitability estimating 89–90; new product development 84–7; product life cycle (PLC) 79–84; product positioning 87–9; prototype development 90–4
profitability, estimating 89–90
promotion *see* communications
prototype development 90–4
public, the 49–51
public relations 24–5
Purdey, Richard 77–8

Regent Models 134–5
reports, market 159–60
retailers 47–9

Sanders, Mark 123
segmentation, market 43
selling, and marketing 26–7
services, and marketing 26–7
services *see* products and services
share, market 68–9
Sinclair C5 35–6
small enterprise 2–4: aid to: information 7–9, 51–2, Loan Guarantee Scheme 201, overseas marketing 156–8, 167–9, product development 91–2; business functions 3, 20–1; definition 21–2; and marketing 4–9
Smiths Crisps 23–4
Society of British Aerospace Companies Ltd 189
strategy, marketing 68; communications 130–3
Street, Brian 214
Strida Ltd 123–6
suppliers 47–9
SWOT (strengths, weaknesses,

222

Index

opportunities, threats) analysis 71–2

tariffs 188–9
technology 44–6: *see also* high technology marketing
Tie-Rack 199–200
Tiefenbrun, Ivor 111–15
Track Sportswear 122–3
Trade and Industry, Department of (DTI) 8, 156–7

Travelway Ltd 66–73

Unipart 60

Walsh, L.S. 161
washing machines 81–4
Wood, John 193
Woods of Windsor 172–7

Young, Lord 7–9